PENNSYLVANIA DUTCH STUFF

DISCARD

PENNSYLVANIA DUTCH STUFF

Pennsylvania Dutch Stuff

A GUIDE TO COUNTRY ANTIQUES

By

Earl F. Robacker

UNIVERSITY OF PENNSYLVANIA PRESS
Philadelphia

Published in Great Britain, India, and Pakistan by the
Oxford University Press
London, Bombay, and Karachi

For Ada

Contents

Illustrations

All photographs by Herman Kartluke

Introduction

PERHAPS you have inherited a solid stone dwelling somewhere down in Pennsylvania; perhaps you have bought a farmhouse in which to spend your summers. Or, perhaps, you are not fortunate enough to be able to live in the leisurely spaciousness of the Dutchland counties, but must build yourself a house in some suburb. You may even have a year-by-year lease on a four-room apartment; but whatever your home you may equip it, if you will, in the manner and with the actual household paraphernalia of the Pennsylvania Dutch of bygone days.

It is not the intention of this book to tell you how to choose your house, or where to build it, or what to pay for it. You will already have decided that, probably about the time you began to think back over those Sunday afternoon drives through the tobacco fields of Lancaster County, past the old Cloisters at Ephrata, or up and down the rolling hills of Bucks or Berks. Perhaps when you stopped your car on the summit of some quiet hill and looked across the misty distances to the Blue Mountain you realized that never again could you be quite content until you, too, owned one of those sturdy farmhouses set in its framework of willow trees, flowing brook, and green meadow. That may even have been the time when, by some act of mental prestidigitation, you transported your house to some real estate development in Connecticut, Wisconsin, or California; at any rate, now you have it, and you want to furnish it in a fitting manner.

You will not need to be told that Sheraton, Hepplewhite, and Savery are out of the question; the salons of Fifty-seventh Street and Madison Avenue will no longer be your hunting grounds. The Pennsylvania Dutch of yesterday were a simple folk and came of peasant ancestry long ago. Their tastes were simple, and such treasures as Philadelphia low-boys and cameo glass, had they had them, would have been no more cherished than their own simple dower chests and their spatterware.

When you begin to furnish your Pennsylvania Dutch house you will want to go to Penn's southeastern counties to do it: to the country sales advertised in the newspapers of a dozen small towns or cities—Nazareth or Annville or Allentown; to the antiques auctions at Reading or Lebanon; to the shows at Bethlehem, Lancaster, or York, as listed in your antiques magazines.

What you buy may not have a pedigree, and you may not be able to run it down in a standard authority. But you will buy it in competition with others who want it badly enough to dispel any doubt in your mind, if such a doubt exists, that it is desirable. And with no name or date to pay for, you will be able to furnish a whole room for the price of a single good Pembroke table—and have more comfort and distinction in your home than your neighbor who is painfully and expensively attempting to create one more precious museum, in which he must dine or sit or lounge with exceeding caution.

There have been many excellent books on furniture, on china, pewter, and glass, but the chances are that you have already discovered that they have little bearing on your present problem, for the simple reason that they were written tor a world that has not taken cognizance of the possibilities of the Pennsylvania Dutchland. Museum pieces in the accepted sense, desirable as they undoubtedly are, would be out of place in your farmhouse, even if you found it expedient to spend the necessary time and money to secure them.

Pennsylvania Dutch "stuff" may not be exactly cheap; too many collectors have been over the ground before you and paid their prices and gone their way for you to play the role of discoverer. Many excellent things have already joined the ranks of the inaccessible. At the same time it is still possible to acquire enough to furnish your Pennsylvania Dutch house with charm and taste, without spending a fortune to do it. You will hear stories of miraculous finds, but such things, as you will discover, usually happen to somebody else, and are not infrequently subject to discount. Yet if you know what to look for and where to go you can ultimately achieve a degree of success that will well repay you for your expenditure of time and energy.

What has been chosen for mention in this book has been selected for its availability and practicality as well as for its decorative value. You may find much, however, that you will not wish to use in your own house, since each dwelling is bound to have its individual problems. You will not need to be afraid to adapt your acquisitions to your own circumstances, because the rules of the game are very simple; Pennsylvania Dutch artistry is a matter of analogy or homogeneity in tone and style rather than of hard and fast periodization in feet, finials, or the like.

Don't try to go back a hundred and fifty years (and that's as far as you *will* be able to go back, with few exceptions) and expect to find all the creature comforts of today. You won't find a really comfortable lounging chair, for example; so after you have acquired enough old objects to enable you to establish an integrated décor for your room, go to your department store and get as simple a chair as you can find and have it upholstered to match your

room.   You'll never regret it.   Similarly, you'll never regret the box springs
and mattress you'll substitute for the ropes on that old bed—and you can
do it without jeopardizing its value as an antique.   More than that, no
matter how beautiful your old clocks may be, it's a good idea to have an
electric one in the kitchen and in the bathroom, just in case.

Again, once you have begun collecting, once the inevitable fervor seizes
you, you may not want to stop until you have *everything* old or everything
Pennsylvania Dutch.   As a curb for that tendency, it is a good idea to keep
in mind the fact that not many Pennsylvania Dutch households ever had
much painted furniture, or a great deal of Stiegel glass, or a great number of
any truly distinctive pieces, for that matter.   Not the least charm is that
which comes through a contrast of the extraordinary with the usual; and
the misguided soul with too great a power of acquisitiveness may find all
too soon that he has too much of even a very good thing.   One good stenciled
rocker may well be more attractive than three, even if you can find three
good ones, and a perfect tea set of Gaudy Dutch can be more effective than
a whole corner cupboard of the same thing.   If you must go in for wholesale
collecting, collect something small enough to be locked out of the way,
where you don't have to look at all of it every day.

Pennsylvania Dutch folk arts have much in common with the primitive
arts of other lands, and if you have already found that Swedish or Danish
or Mexican wares are of more than passing interest, you will discover that
they combine quite effectively with Pennsylvania things.   In homes where
it would be folly to discard perfectly good conventional furniture it is still
possible to achieve distinction by displaying colorful painted tin, fractur
(pen and ink drawings) or chinaware as an accent, whether its provenance
happens to be American or European.   For that matter, not everything that
is typically Pennsylvania Dutch originated in Pennsylvania, as will appear
later.   Still, you will wish to know just what is Pennsylvania Dutch and
what is not, particularly since imitators are at work, and since more than
one unwary collector has discovered that what he bought for early American
glass has turned out to be late Mexican.

This volume will not pile documentation upon documentation to prove
points of purely historical interest, nor will it in any case presume to deliver
the "last word."   What it will attempt to do is to provide enough accurate
information for you to be able to choose confidently and intelligently when
you go out to buy, and to furnish your house in the way you wish to do it—
in the Pennsylvania Dutch manner.

People and Patterns

THE first "Pennsylvania Dutch," that is, emigrants from the Rhineland and from Switzerland, came to America as early as the time of William Penn in 1683. Many of them were desperately poor, and few were affluent enough to bring more possessions than their sea chests would accommodate. Eager to escape from the persecutions following the religious wars that had so often devastated their homeland, they asked of the New World no more than a chance to start life over again.

Beginning with the arrival of the first few colonists on the *Concord*, sometimes referred to as "the *Mayflower* of the Pennsylvania Dutch," they proceeded to entrench themselves in the farming region to the north and west of Philadelphia. Since they had brought so little with them—indeed, many of them had sold themselves into a condition of bondage to pay for their very passage—they were obliged to secure all their worldly possessions in the new country by the efforts of their own hands. Remembering the dwellings of the homeland and the arts that had been cherished there, they adapted the ways of the old life to the exigencies of the new with peculiar success.

They were, from the very beginning, a people apart. They spoke a different tongue, a condition which in itself did not make for popularity with the English and the Scotch-Irish of the new Colony, particularly since more and more Germans put in their appearance with the passing years. Then, too, they tended to maintain and defend the peculiar religious beliefs which had been one of the principal causes of their persecution in Europe. More than that, they showed comparatively little interest in the political or social affairs of the Colony, but concerned themselves instead with developing what was to become one of the finest farming regions of America.

The upshot of this tendency was that with the passing of time rather less was known of the vast Pennsylvania Dutchland than more, and succeeding generations of English-speaking citizens regarded the German element as strange, unsocial, and obstinate. To what extent the opinion of the outside world was correct is not within the province of this book to determine, but that world was at least partly wrong. Suffice it to say here that during the eighteenth century, and well into the nineteenth, there developed in this "backward" section one of the most interesting and most individual folk

4

cultures that America has seen—unknown and unnoticed because the people and the land were so consistently ignored except as the outside world benefited by the choice country produce that found its way to Philadelphia or Baltimore in the great farm wagons of the "Dutch."

Deep in the rural sections, that is to say from Philadelphia northward to Easton and beyond, and westward toward Pittsburgh, descendants of the old peasant stock were creating generous farmsteads, mighty barns, and sturdy houses, evidences of their steadily increasing prosperity. And, once the day of the earliest privations had passed, there came into being that manifold variety of household gear so eagerly sought after by the collector of today.

As might be expected, the very earliest furniture, for all its ponderous weight and substance, has largely disappeared. The collector seeking to furnish his home with the rude pieces of earliest times might do well to reflect that even the Pennsylvania Dutch, who in that day knew little and cared less about the fine art of cabinetmaking, were glad in time to relegate their cumbersome homemade efforts to the summer kitchen, the cellar, and the outhouses. To be sure, occasional meritorious pieces of the period are to be seen in the larger museums and in the possession of various historical societies, but for all their historical value they are hardly decorative additions to the houses of today. What may be considered as "typical" Pennsylvania Dutch furniture is that which was created after the problems of food, clothing, and shelter had ceased to be of primary and immediate importance. By the early 1800's the people as a class were well on the way to affluence, and it is in the period of, perhaps, 1785 to 1860 that the Pennsylvania Dutch decorative arts came into their own.

Instead of the fine mahogany pieces which the Philadelphia cabinetmakers executed with such devotion to line and detail, the Pennsylvania Dutch craftsman—who was also perforce carpenter, cooper, dairyman, teamster, and jack-of-all-trades—turned to his limestone acres and selected walnut for his best efforts. He found also that the cherry which grew in such abundance was almost as good as mahogany, and that for special effects tiger-striped and bird's-eye maple left nothing to be desired. On these he worked with care and precision, sometimes in an effort to copy the work of professional artists in the medium, but just as often according to remembered patterns from his former homeland.

Such "good" pieces were not ordinarily painted, but the everyday chairs, tables, and chests of pine and poplar, so much more easily worked than hardwood, were thoroughly coated with pigment in bold colors, probably at the behest of his wife. Little did he dream that the restless children of a later generation would have no peace until they had laboriously scraped and dissolved away the covering he had applied, in their zeal to get to the naked wood. Unadorned surfaces must have been abhorrent to the Pennsylvania farmers, who made up for their lack of professional achievement in the details of cabinet-making by their thoroughness in applying color, sometimes with garish effect, sometimes with small consideration for proportion, but always with a distinctive touch.

But it is the decorative devices employed in superimposed ornamentation that gives Pennsylvania Dutch work its greatest distinction, greater than the arresting use of strong color or the soft sheen of cherry or walnut. These motifs have been the subject of clamorous concern to many present-day writers, some of whom have discovered and repeatedly proclaimed what has always been evident to the art student, that it is foreign rather than native in inspiration. Such writers point first to Pennsylvania Dutch artistry and then to the fabrics of Sweden and Denmark, the furniture of Switzerland, and the pottery of Germany, and forthwith deny the right of paternity to anything this side of the Atlantic almost down to contemporary times. To these, and to those who immediately rally to the defense of the native provenance of their heirlooms and acquisitions, one must say with the landlord in *Silas Marner*, "The truth lies a'tween ye."

Certainly Pennsylvania Dutch artistry is foreign in inspiration. What Colonial artistry was not? Cut off forever from his homeland and native fireside, the Dutchman would have been a strange person indeed had he not tended, in a not-too-friendly New World, to gather about him reminders of the past and turn his homesickness into a pleasant nostalgia. And in drawing on the past he tapped a considerable reservoir of talent, for in the composite this Pennsylvania Dutchman was German, Swiss, Huguenot, and Welsh, with an occasional smattering of Scotch-Irish, Holland Dutch, and other strains.

One striking factor in the case is the degree of reluctance with which he came to make use of the new country as a source of inspiration for his art forms. Certainly it was no lack of industry; his material possessions bore witness to that. Neither was it a lack of unborn talent, for why should not a race which counted eminent scholars and divines among its numbers at the outset and later gave to the world famous scientists, physicians, lawyers, statesmen, generals, and even a president also have turned out a celebrated artist or two somewhere along the line? It was simply a case of putting other things first; of placing the affairs of the world in one category and the things of the heart and the home in another. When the artists eventually did arrive it was after the inevitable amalgamation of the Dutchland with the rest of the country had begun, and some of the sharp points of the original tastes had been rubbed off by the influences of the New World. Even so, the first artistic creations were not always purely European in character; the new tools and new media alone would take care of that, and as the years went on the leveling influences of assimilation worked to such an extent that the home decoration of the Dutchland was essentially that of America.

Among the decorative devices which connected Dutch Pennsylvania with the Old World, in what might be called a state of symbiosis, the tulip probably stands first.   Perhaps the tulipomania of the Netherlands and of Europe was responsible for that; perhaps it goes farther back—to Persia, as one writer maintains, or at least to a pre-European origin.   It is quite possible that the tulip of dower chest, pottery, cooky cutter, and spatterware preceded the dooryard flower to Pennsylvania homesteads, for it is to be found on the very earliest of authenticated objects, in composition and structural detail like those of the homeland.   Another device traced to Persia is the exotic pomegranate, so often found on bride's boxes.   No more native to Pennsylvania than they were to Germany, pomegranates are still typically Pennsylvania Dutch in the sense that in this country they are commonly found in Pennsylvania Dutch representation and nowhere else.   Pomegranate flowers, incidentally, are frequently confused with tulips, to which in profile on bride's boxes they are not dissimilar.

Representative of the country also is the heart, whether low and broad-lobed or tall and slightly more symmetrical.   So well-loved was this pattern that it was employed wherever the artist could find a good place to put it— on birth and baptismal certificates, in fractur, in needlework, on dower chests, in wood, in tin, and in iron.   Is it the sacred heart of Christian symbolism?   There are those who would have it so.   Whatever its original significance, it is a pleasing device, and its presence on an object of otherwise hard-to-determine provenance will almost automatically indicate a Pennsylvania Dutch origin.

The angel is another characteristic ornamentation, and may have its source in the same religious zeal that fired the first settlers and brought them to this country.   Angels hover on birth certificates and are to be found on certain types of painted furniture and in cooky cutters.   Naïve in execution, they might be called caricatures if it were not evident that their creators took them seriously.   It has been suggested that they are descended from the patterns of the illuminated manuscripts of medieval times, and when illumination became one of the lost arts (disappearing in Pennsylvania by way of fractur and pen drawings) they persisted because of their spiritual connotations.   This feeling is found also in the reluctance of the Pennsylvania Dutch to destroy a worn-out Bible.   "Leave it be," they say.   "After I'm gone somebody else can burn it."

The star is another device popular in decoration.   It is not peculiar to the Dutchland, but is used with telling effect on dower chests, on quilts and other forms of needlecraft, and in punched tin work.   It was a much admired pattern on the spatterware made in England for the Pennsylvania trade. Is there any point in suggesting that the star indicates a religious symbolism as yet not clearly traced? Perhaps not, considering the far-flung use of star motifs over the face of the earth. To be bluntly realistic about the whole matter of Pennsylvania Dutch art, the people admired certain patterns, whether tulip, pomegranate, angel, or star, and used them over and over again without consideration of any esoteric significance, but just because they liked them.

They liked peafowl, the peacock especially. The well-to-do had them around the farmyard because of their brilliant colors, and rich and not-so-rich (there seem to have been no poor families) liked seeing them on their tableware, on tin trays, and on paper. Those who go in for tracking down the Original Cause of the popularity of this regal bird will probably encounter serious obstacles in ascribing a predilection for anything smacking of royalty to the Pennsylvania Dutch, who had good reason for hating the very sound of the word. They liked other birds, too, especially the *distelfink* (goldfinch) and the salad bird (wild canary). The flashing color of the parrot made him a favorite, not only in the kitchen cage but in pen paintings and on tinware. The robin, the thrush, the dove, and the eagle had their places as well, to say nothing of the rooster.

The rose was a favorite, as it has been ever since there were roses. The variation in form and composition is somewhat less than might be expected, though there are cabbage roses, moss roses, King's and Queen's roses and Adams roses. What has come to be called the Adams rose, a bloom shown in profile, was pressed into service in a surprising number of ways, almost always to good effect. Painted and stenciled furniture, china and glassware, miniature boxes, needle-work, clock faces, especially the wag-on-the-wall type, and fractur designs attest to the love for this universal flower. Nor was the rose alone cherished. Fuchsias and dahlias, primroses and daffodils, dogwood and morning-glories—none of them exactly shrinking or modest— brightened the corners where they were. Their effects were bold rather than subtle, but their purpose of adding color to otherwise barren and unrelieved surfaces was well served. Let it be urged again that the collector would do well to tread lightly in this territory, and not over-do the number of his floral acquisitions. In spite of the prevailing opinion to the contrary, the Pennsylvania Dutch did not make a practice of cramming their rooms with painted pieces, and those who do so today may rightly blame only themselves when bemoaning the resultant cluttered effect.

Flowers in urns or vases show a close resemblance to one another, and indicate a common origin, perhaps going back to China by way of England and Persia, whether by sea lanes or overland caravan routes. The panels of dower chests, Gaudy Dutch china, and punched tin coffee pots frequently utilized this motif, and there is a variation, possibly a refinement, of it in some of the better pen drawings of Ephrata.

Horses, so vital a part of the agricultural economy of the land, also came in for attention as an art form, whether atop the barn to show the way the winds of the Dutchland were blowing, or on cooky cutters or on sgraffito plates, in which case they usually served as mounts for hunters or warriors. The deer seems to have been the only other animal thus well beloved, judging by the evidences at hand. The deer of Salopian may possibly explain why this particular form of chinaware, in other ways not especially calculated to please the Pennsylvanians, found a place in the corner cupboard.

Delineations of fruit are both characteristic and colorful. Housewives loved the rich glow of strawberries on their strawberry china; of melons, peaches, plums, and cherries on their stenciled furniture; of oranges and apples in their plaster ornaments. The fruit plates and fruit-carved furniture of Victorian times found immediate acceptance in the lowland counties. The tomato-like fruits on painted tôleware are as Dutch as can be. For once, at least, remembering the framed Victorian "dining room" colored prints beginning with a life-sized, split watermelon and ending at any improbable point beyond that, one is inclined to credit the Pennsylvania Dutch with more or less decorative restraint, after all.

A good specimen of imitative art is the house design, showing a simple square building in partial perspective. In spatterware it is called a schoolhouse; in fractur, with smoke belching furiously from the chimneys, it is just a house, though possibly a stone house, at that.

The geometrically-shaped barn signs, sometimes called *hexafus* or witch symbols, have been discussed in print ably and often. Now and then they are also to be found indoors, on knife racks, comb cases, or sometimes inside the covers of books. These have been searched out so thoroughly that the average collector has but little chance of discovering one.

Where for any reason actual designs were not employed on large surfaces, such as those of furniture, the Dutch artisan had recourse to at least two other methods. One of these was to spatter the surface either completely or in part, by using a sponge dipped in colored paint. Now and then two or even three colors were so used. This practice was followed also in Connecticut, and may have been picked up from cabinetworkers who moved from there to Pennsylvania. The second method, which was actually supplementary rather than complete in most cases, was that of drawing bands across edges too narrow to admit of any pattern. The legs and arms of chairs were so treated. The colors used were ordinarily yellow or black, and once in a while black bands were also used on chair legs to suggest the joints of bamboo.

The "tree of life" motif should certainly be mentioned at this point, not only for its beauty but because, like the pomegranate and the urn, it shows an important kinship with the art of Persia, where it reached its finest expression in rugs. At the hands of the Pennsylvania artist the pattern was usually developed as a straight central stem with curved branches or fronds on either side, sometimes so symmetrical as to suggest segments of concentric circles. The pattern had a special interpretation in the fine work done at the Ephrata Cloisters, where the artists used flowers as well as branches to convey a mystic symbolism. It is found on door towels and samplers, in cut-paper work, in fractur, and more rarely on painted surfaces.

Chairs and Benches

OUTSTANDING among the furniture which the collector will wish to acquire is that which is known simply as stenciled, or, more commonly, "painted." The term carries a fuller meaning than is at once evident, however, since the painting was much more than a mere utilitarian process, and serves as a generic designation for the chairs, settees, chests, and other wooden pieces decorated in floral, fruit, and other motifs according to a more or less variable formula.

Chairs may be mentioned first, not only because the collector frequently thinks of chairs rather early in his quest, but because, more than in the case of any other article of furniture, good specimens may still be found among the shops of country dealers. It is as well to state at the outset for the benefit of the amateur that he will do considerably better to begin with the dealers than to try to gain access to private homes in the hope of bearing away treasures for a song. The dealers have been over the entire territory many times, and have bought for resale most of what may be secured at anything like a reasonable price. Old furniture still in the hands of its original owners is usually there because the owners treasure it; and it is likely to remain there because the repeated visits of buyers have only too often tended to give it a supposed worth far in excess of its actual market value.

Naturally, most collectors like the idea of getting chairs by sets, usually for use in dining rooms, and it is by no means impossible to do so. At the same time, it is foolish to pass up a pair of good chairs, or even a single good one, when no more are to be had, since they can frequently be used with a desk, in a bedroom, or a sun room. There is always the remote chance, too, of finding others to match, although matching is becoming increasingly difficult. Sets of eight or twelve are not unknown, but they should be very closely compared to be sure that they really do match. This is particularly true in instances where one or more of the set happens to be badly worn. Six is the standard set. "Sets" of four or five are occasionally offered for sale, but unless the collector has a special use for these numbers he should realize that the chances of resale are less with these unconventional sets.

Painted chairs, like most other pieces of painted furniture, are an expression of the well-known Pennsylvania Dutch love for color. Structurally they are simple and substantial, usually with no side arms, no excess turning and no carving. Workmanly in construction, they were built first of all for long, hard use, and only secondarily to serve as ornaments to otherwise rather severely furnished rooms. Variations in structure are to be found, with no particular superiority in any one form; the desirability of the piece lies not so much in its beauty of line as in its decoration.

Balloon backs, so called because of the supposed resemblance of the back to the profile of an inflated balloon, are often sought after because they depart from the more or less conventional straight-backed forms. Taller than many others, and often with a difference of as much as two inches of added distance from floor to seat, they show to particular advantage in large rooms. In fact, a set of six colorful balloon backs in any room other than a fairly large one might prove a trifle overpowering. The back of the usual balloon chair has a broad central splat, rising to meet the curved or ballooned portion connecting the posts. The seats are of wood, usually pine or some other soft wood, as is the case with most of the Pennsylvania Dutch painted chairs.

Arrow backs were as popular in Pennsylvania as they were elsewhere along the Seaboard. They received their name from the fact that the shaved round spindles of the back were flattened and shaped near the top to indicate roughly the outline of an arrowhead. Many of the painted chairs were backed with simply turned spindles, sometimes in combination with one or more horizontal slats. Others had a broad, vertical central splat, frequently gracefully shaped, rising to meet a broad slat at the top. In any case the stenciled decoration was applied to the largest available surface or surfaces, except the seats, though seats were sometimes partly decorated.

As for the decorations themselves, they existed in almost endless variety, the possibilities being limited chiefly by the imaginative capacity of the artist. On a background of green, yellow, or brown (in the latter case not infrequently "grained" to suggest the natural markings of wood, walnut for instance) stenciled designs were applied, attempts usually being made at a kind of symmetry.

One favorite combination was a grouping of fruit in natural colors, with one or more birds hovering or perched above, the whole design being judiciously accented with gilt. Cherries, grapes, and plums are often found in such fruit combinations, either closely clustered in a central position, or repeated across the top of the splat. The shell-and-peach combination was a favorite pattern. A conventional gilded or painted border usually framed the composition.

Flower combinations occur with equal frequency, and where, as is often the case, time has softened the original coloring somewhat, the result is usually pleasing. The favorite flower seems to have been the rose, oftenest in a strong tone of pink with modulations of darker and lighter tones, as well as of white. Sometimes, when a rose motif was used in the center, other flowers were used at the ends, either in a conventionalized form or in a more or less natural representation. Four-petaled flowers like those of the dogwood occur very often, and in varying colors. Morning-glories made a popular and effective decoration. The horn-of-plenty was used in combination with both flowers and fruit.

Telling results were often achieved when the original stenciled design was touched up by the artist's brush, and, while devotees of stenciled furniture hesitate to say so, some of the most attractive pieces seem to have been done entirely by hand. One such group is a set of six straight-backed chairs, slightly smaller than usual, in a dark brown color grained in a good imitation of walnut. The central decoration of the broad top is a single rose, shading from deep pinky red to white, and set in a cluster of dark green leaves. Another cluster of white-petaled flowers at each end supplies balance. In the wide central panel appears a bunch of brightly colored cherries, a little darker than the rose above. Panel, splat, seat, and posts are boldly outlined with bands of deep, creamy white, which was probably originally yellow. There is no indication that any gilding had ever been used. The original brush strokes show quite plainly. This set of chairs is stamped "George Hay, Chair Cabinet & Coffin Maker, York, Pa.," a circumstance which is unusual, since few Pennsylvania artisans signed their work. Cabinetmakers, incidentally, were also frequently coffinmakers. Another known fancy chair artist was one who identified himself as "Joseph Jones—nearly opposite Academy, West Chester, Pa."

How much of the original paint the collector should expect to find is a moot point. Few sets in anything like perfect condition are to be had, of course, and when one is known to exist there is likely to be a waiting list of prospective buyers. One Pennsylvania dealer claims to have supplied a millionaire client with six such sets a number of years ago, but has not been able to find a single one since. Certainly, since the collector is presumably buying for the sake of the ornamentation as much as for the chair he should not allow himself to be talked into buying articles so badly damaged that he will be able to take little pride in his acquisition. On the other hand, if he waits until a perfect set comes along he may never get any at all.

Then, too, there is the problem of redecoration. Painted decorations may have been touched up last year or forty years ago. If the whole piece shows a fine tracery of time checks, nothing short of a chemical analysis could tell definitely whether the original owner had had his favorite chairs brightened up. But if the flowers bloom freshly on a worn and faded background, if they are thick or tacky to the touch, if there is a marked discrepancy in tone between the ornamentation of two chairs in the same set—

then the buyer should think twice before he pays more than the price of a reproduction.

The wonder is that so much of the pristine coloring should have been preserved at all, considering the usage that chairs often get, though it is just as well, perhaps, that the garish hues of red cherries, green leaves, blue plums, and striped melons on a yellow background have been subdued by the hand of time. The secret of the preservation lies in the fact that very often the chairs were not used at all, but were kept in darkened best rooms, just "for fancy," and in addition were often swathed in coverings to give them still further protection. It is said that a certain old lady cherished in this manner for more than fifty years the set she had originally received from her father as a wedding present.

Developed in rural districts as it was, the painted furniture of Pennsylvania is essentially crude. As such it cannot be expected to mix well with more sophisticated articles. It loses luster by being combined even with the Hitchcock chairs of New England, for instance, though it will blend harmoniously with practically any wood that can be finished in its natural color, with the possible exception of some of the modern bleached woods.

Essentially similar to painted chairs in construction and treatment is the "Dutch bench," or wooden settee, a most desirable acquisition for a sun room, a large hall, a recreation room, or a covered terrace, where it need not be expected to double for the far more comfortable modern davenport. Like the painted chairs, the settee has a plank seat, usually in one piece, which measures up to an inch and a half in thickness, eighteen or twenty inches in depth and seven feet in length. It is seldom possible to match chairs and settee, even if one wanted to do so; indeed, there seems to be little reason to suppose that they were intended to go together in sets, for all their similarity. Arrow backs (that is, those in which the spindles of the back are shaped like those of the arrow-backed chairs) are often considered to be the most desirable, either because of the additional amount of handwork they indicate, or because of the pleasing simplicity of the design. In construction Dutch settees are braced with four or more posts at the back, across which the broad central splat and a narrower one several inches above the seat are fastened. The spindles, whether arrow-shaped or simply turned, are usually set between the lower splat and the seat. In exceptional cases, spindles rise directly from the seat to a top rail.

After the spindles, the arms claim the attention of the buyer, since their shape may either relieve or accentuate the essential massiveness of the whole. Gracefully curving arms, each ending in a simple scroll which is firmly braced by a strong spindle or post rising from the seat, are desirable, but not essential. Simple arms, terminating with no attempt at decoration, may be better proportioned than an over-ambitious curve which succeeds only in

CHARACTERISTIC DUTCH BENCH

BURL MAHOGANY CHEST

giving a heavy, Victorian effect. The top rail of these benches was sometimes shaped to give the effect of several chairs set side by side. The resulting design was often quite effective in its combination of straight edge and simple, cut-out curvature, which frequently suggest the shape of a heart.

It would be foolish to try to establish a standard for such benches; they were individually made, and in their finished form represented not so much a copy from a book of patterns as the distinctive conception of the maker. They are so strikingly individual in comparison with primitive furniture forms developed elsewhere in the country that a good specimen can easily dominate, as well as determine the central motif for, an entire room.

As in the case of chairs, it is the imposed ornamentation which gives the Dutch bench most of its choiceness, since at best it is hardly a thing of comfort. What has been said of chair decoration is fundamentally true here, except that it is far less easy to find specimens with all the original stenciling intact—to say nothing of the fact that the settee is not the easiest article of furniture to find at all. If the buyer discovers a bench sound in construction and possessing a reasonable amount of the old paint, he could do worse than take it along with him. Far less satisfactory would be the alternative of picking up for little more than the price of a chair a freshly puttied and painted bench "good enough for the terrace." In any event the home owner will probably wish to provide a seat covering and cushions for comfort, and perhaps throw a small coverlet or hooked rug over the back, none of which need in the least detract from the charm of the original.

Less easy to find and consequently higher in price are these same settees in miniature, or in child sizes. Usually made as play furniture, they display a degree of expertness in their decoration not always lavished on larger pieces. An unusually attractive one in which the floral patterns appear on a red background has been discovered but, as in the case of the parent article, the general color favorite seems to have been a dark, warm brown. As a utilitarian object, a bench not more than two feet over all would undoubtedly not be found near the top of the buyer's list of "musts," but with the increasing scarcity of painted furniture of all kinds in Pennsylvania, it would be a hardy buyer who would feel that he could afford to pass one up.

Painted rocking chairs also show manifestations of Pennsylvania Dutch decorative skill, and, even if one feels he has no immediate need for such a chair, he will find it hard to resist a gaily painted array of birds, fruit or flowers, or all three on an armed rocker of the Boston type, or on the armless "sewing" or "nursing" variety. There is apt to be considerable variation in the skill of execution of these chairs. Not all of them are comfortable, and, if the buyer plans to sit in his chair, he should try it out first. Are the spindles of the back set in a curve rather than straight across? One would hardly wish to use a covering of any kind, as he might with a settee, no matter how much more endurable the spindles might become thereby. Is the weight of the back fairly proportioned to that of the rest of the chair? If not, it will tilt back disconcertingly.

Rocking chairs require more space than their straight brethren, especially if they are of the balloon back type. The apartment dweller might find even a small chair unwieldy, although in the broad stone houses of Pennsylvania that problem would probably never occur. While with painted furniture the question of age is not especially significant, rocking chairs in which the rocker is set into the legs, rather than the legs into the rocker, are usually both earlier and more distinctive.

Now and then a strongly individualistic piece thrusts itself upon the attention of the buyer, whose reaction may range from a startled and immediate rejection to an equally strong urge toward acquisition. In this class should undoubtedly be placed the settee rocker, that ingenious device which enabled a mother to cradle her child and rock it to sleep, while she herself worked at her sewing or perhaps shelled peas for the family dinner. The distinctive feature of this settee, which was ordinarily smaller than the usual stationary type, was the fact that the small spindles of the back were continued part way around the front, enclosing enough of the plank seat to provide a commodious cradle. The enclosed portion, seldom more than a foot high, was finished off with a neatly turned rail. In a good state of preservation these rocking settees, particularly when their floral decorations are intact, are striking looking pieces of furniture.

A piece which the buyer will probably find more expensive than even a rather good chair is the lowly four-legged footstool. Perhaps no more than a few were ever made, or perhaps the stenciled decorations on their tops were so soon obliterated by usage that they lost their desirability; at any rate they appear so infrequently that many collectors have never been able to acquire one. Typical specimens are about eight to ten inches in height, oval in shape, and contain a cluster of fruit and leaves on the surface of the two-inch plank top, with one or more lines of solid color at the edge. Brown is the usual color for these stools.

While painted or stenciled chairs, benches, and stools may be the most distinctive among such household articles, they are by no means the only ones that possess a characteristic Pennsylvania Dutch flavor. More than that, as has already been suggested, there is a certain danger in having too many of them unless they are relieved by less striking furniture to act as a neutral ground, or foil. Of course, if the original colors have been toned down by age, the matter may be of less concern, but even so there is a merit which comes from contrast.

Once away from the painted ornamentation, the buyer is faced, in most shops, with a rather ordinary array of chairs, none of which at first seems to possess any particular distinction. Ladder-backs and Windsors may be found now and then, but, since they are essentially similar to New England types, the buyer may wish to look for something more typically Pennsylvanian. One answer to the problem is in the low, semi-circular-backed barroom chair, which, in addition to its distinctive shape, is reasonably comfortable. Such chairs are particularly effective when paired, as before a fireplace, or at either side of a bay window, and their compactness makes them ideal for use with bridge tables or on porches or terraces. Like painted furniture, they are very solidly built. Common characteristics are the curved back, which tapers sidewise and forward to form the arm, which in turn curves downward to act as a forepost; turned spindles sloping gently backward and reaching from the seat to the upper frame; and stout legs well braced with wooden rungs and often reinforced with heavy wire or even metal rods. While such chairs may be painted, either to harmonize with the dominant color of the room or to pick up a subordinate one, they are perhaps most effective in the rich tones of the natural wood. While pine, poplar, or some other soft wood was usually used for the plank seat, rungs and spindles seem to have been fashioned from whatever hard woods were at hand, with hickory and oak predominating.

Variants among barroom chairs are chiefly those forms which have the back built up to a greater height, as in the Pennsylvania "grandfather's" chair, or those which by greater length of spindle and bow back approach the Windsor types. While identical forms look well either by themselves or in combination with stenciled or painted furniture, the effect is less happy when barroom variants are employed in combination. Since the comparatively low-backed forms with spindles of even height seem to be easiest to secure, they are usually the collector's first choice when more than one is needed for any particular purpose.

Then, of course, there are the cane-seated wooden chairs, restrained forms of which may often be used in combination with the sturdier plank bottoms, with good effect. The collector will do well to acquire his painted chairs first and delay the purchase of cane seats until he can feel sure that their lighter construction and sometimes elaborately turned spindles and rungs will not clash with the simplicity of the painted furniture, and reduce the whole scheme to mediocrity.

The various heavy wood boxes, wood box seats, and high-backed settles offered by dealers, while distinctive and authentic in themselves, seldom mix well with objects of greater refinement. It is not just old furniture that the discriminating householder wishes to collect; it is the best he can secure of the really representative and therefore desirable pieces of the period he is trying to re-create.

Cupboards

No enthusiast for the things of Dutch Pennsylvania will long be content until he has acquired one of the magnificent cupboards that once adorned the great kitchens of the stone houses. True, he will find the modern refrigerator and built-in storage units of all kinds better suited to the demands of his own kitchen than the capacious giant of the past, but there is a cupboard for dining room, living room, or study, and in sizes and shapes to suit the most discriminating.

Perhaps it is well that the prospective buyer cannot see at one time the array of interesting and imposing cupboards that have been offered for sale within the past ten or twenty years, for he might lose heart and jump to the conclusion that everything good has already found its way into some private collection. It is true, of course, that the newcomer to the field of Pennsylvania Dutch antiques has arrived rather late as far as garnering museum pieces is concerned, but that it is not *too* late a canvass of the shops of the dealers and of the auction rooms will speedily show.

The most distinctive piece that the searcher could hope to secure would undoubtedly be the almost fabulous painted cupboard from the Mahontongo Valley of southeastern Pennsylvania, and for the sheer distinction of such a piece he would have to part company with a very formidable sum of money. Not much information as to the genesis of the Mahontongo Valley furniture is at hand. One story is that an early race of cabinetmakers migrated from Connecticut to this secluded valley in times gone by (and just how long ago no one seems to be willing to say) bringing with them a knowledge of decorative painting unknown in Pennsylvania up to that time. Another tale is that the painted bureaus and cupboards which eventually came to the dealers' mart were an indigenous product, portraying in their painted figures evidences of an intricate and involved symbolism purely and anciently Germanic. There are even those who profess to find in the imagery of a single bureau a mysterious "key" to all the ornamental devices so universally employed throughout the Dutchland. Still another story is that the furniture was created by one Jacob Mäser, who is also said to have produced excellent dower chests. Whatever the truth of the matter, it cannot be denied that the fortunate possessor of such a cupboard has a piece which is the envy of the entire collecting fraternity.

As was indicated earlier, a great deal of the oldest Pennsylvania furniture was heavy and cumbersome to an extent which would minimize its desirability in any house other than one comparable to the commodious dwellings of the past.   Such a statement would naturally apply to the great cupboards which in an earlier day had to do duty for the modern set-up of kitchen cabinets, china closets, multifarious built-in units and the like.   Still, for all its size—and one notable specimen stands six feet ten inches in height and is six feet eight inches in width—a Mahontongo Valley sideboard would undoubtedly justify the creation of a special place for it, even to the point of building in a recessed space at the end or side of a dining room.

The cupboard referred to has two doors of six glass panes each in the upper part, the doors being separated by a unique three-pane glass panel. The top of the cabinet is what is known to the trade as "molded" or corniced, and fluted quarter columns adorn the corners.   The upper framework of the doors and of the central panel is ornamented with eight painted stars in pink, red, and blue.   The lower part of the cupboard has two sunken panel doors bearing the painted figures of angels, above which, on each door, appears the cryptic word "Concortia."   There are two drawers above the doors, each decorated with birds and tulips, and a painted panel in between, bearing a large tulip over the date, 1830.   The doors are hung with H-hinges, and the feet are ogee.

The average collector, however, will have to content himself with something far less unusual, since but a relatively small number of Mahontongo Valley pieces of any kind are known to exist.   Just plain "Dutch" cupboards, comparable to the Mahontongo Valley variety in size and general style are to be found, some of them very early.   The doors may contain nine panes of glass rather than six, and even twelve are not unknown.   There will be variations in molding, in corner reeding or fluting, and in the feet, according to the age of the piece, or according to the fancy of the cabinetmaker.   More sought after than the H-hinges, by some buyers, are the early rat-tail variety. Cupboards may be of walnut, of cherry, or of soft wood.   All the varying degrees of skill from the obviously homemade product of the carpenter-farmer to the masterly execution of the cabinetmaker appear, with a corresponding price range, of course.

If any particular wood is demanded, the buyer will often have to scrape through successive layers of paint, sometimes almost unbelievably thick, in order to find out just what it was that the builder started with.   Dutch housewives were famous for being good housekeepers, and apparently one way of keeping the kitchen cupboard in good trim was to add a coat of bright paint of a new color whenever signs of wear or dinginess appeared.

Usually the only thing to do is to get rid of all the old paint, and start from scratch.   There is one exception, however, and that is in the case of what dealers call simply "old blue," a soft, rather darkly grayed blue which seems to have been a popular color from the very earliest times.   The visitor to the American Wing of the Metropolitan Museum in New York will see this blue on woodwork taken from a fine, early Pennsylvania dwelling.   If one is fortunate enough to come across this blue paint he should make every effort to preserve it, both for its innate attractiveness and as an indication of the age of the article which bears it.   Conversely, the bugbear of those who refinish old furniture is the "Dutch red" which was so lavishly applied to furniture of every kind, fifty or more years ago.   This red paint possessed a penetrating quality almost unknown to modern science, and its pigment seems to linger on in cherry and walnut after the paint itself has gone, somewhat in the manner of the smile of Lewis Carroll's Cheshire cat.

One of the most original among peculiarly Pennsylvania Dutch cupboards is the large, sturdy variety which has been "spattered."   Such cupboards in themselves usually possess no particular virtue in design, but were obviously built to accommodate as great as possible a number of dishes, glassware, pots and pans, and the like.   The spatter which lends them distinction is an all-over painted decoration applied by hand with a sponge moistened with paint, as a final protective and adorning coat.   This gives an effect of stippling, sometimes plain, sometimes with a markedly rhythmic arrangement of sponge strokes.   The spattering process is one not necessarily limited to furniture, or even to Pennsylvania, but appears here to an extent which marks it as a rule rather than an exception.

The colors chosen by the artist are not always those which have the greatest appeal for moderns, since the ultimate effect, after the passing of years, is usually a brick red.   Perhaps the most frequent combination is yellow sponged on a red background, with the yellow now softened consier-d ably in tone from its brightly primal hue.   Black is also used for this mottled effect.   If the sponging was originally employed to carry out a definite motif, there is little evidence of such an intention today, although there may well be collectors who in the past have obtained such pieces.   Door panels usually match each other, and sometimes there is an obvious attempt at uniformity elsewhere, but the entire process is usually characterized by a haphazard simplicity.

Of course, any piece obviously belonging to what has come to be called the "Painted Period" is worth a collector's notice.   However, with spatter cupboards as with stenciled chairs, the home-owner will need to exercise a certain amount of discretion in displaying a given piece, for so unusual an article may well dominate an entire room, whether the purchaser had intended to make it a focal point or not.   Curiously enough, this primitive stippling was ordinarily confined to the largest cupboards, perhaps because a large, unrelieved expanse of solid color was at variance with the Dutch love for ornamentation. Small spattered objects, such as semi-occasional boxes, to say nothing of Staffordshire spatterware, usually display a finer degree of skill.

More useful to many collectors than a cupboard with glazed or wooden doors is the open "Welsh" dresser, which lends itself so well to displaying china, pewter, or glass. The fine condition in which these dressers can still be found may be explained by the fact that they have been subjected to less rigorous use than the closed variety, their owners very probably having used them principally for ornamental purposes. Structurally, the lower part of these cupboards is the same as that of the closed type. The top, however, consists of a series of shelves running its entire width. Sometimes these shelves are successively narrower toward the top, but as often they are of the same width, especially when the top of the dresser is scalloped or neatly corniced by an architectural molding.

Perhaps as good a guide as any in indicating the desirability of the Welsh dresser is the amount of skill that has gone into its execution. While it is possible to trace Sheraton influence in some unusually choice specimens, and to draw analogies in moldings, reeding, and feet to the work of well-known cabinetmakers, the appeal of most of these country pieces lies rather in their sturdy, honest proportions. Hardwood cupboards naturally offered more opportunities to display good workmanship than pine or poplar, and, happily, a walnut or cherry dresser is within the bounds of possibility for most collectors. Prices are apt to be in pretty close ratio to the amount of hand labor that was expended by the artisan, sometimes admittedly without particular reference to the final effect. A turned apron at the bottom; a turned board below the top molding; an ogee or cyma curve on the edges of sides or shelves; slits at the front of shelves to accommodate spoons; an extra drawer or two; recessed panels—all these contribute to a finished appearance, and increase the value (or valuation) of the object accordingly.

As for the actual proportions of the cupboard, the buyer will be guided by his individual needs. Late examples, which tend toward being rather narrow, are perhaps less pleasing than the real old-time article, as broad as it was high. Different sizes have their respective merits, of course, and the fine walnut dresser which would do credit to the dining room might well be out of place in, say, a play room, bar, or sun porch, where simple pine would be more in keeping.

For many people the corner cupboard has a charm not to be found in any other type, and luckily the supply has so far seemed large enough to meet the demand. Practically every early house must have had at least one, to judge from the vast variety which have found their way to the sales rooms. It is true, of course, that unless they are of heroic proportions their triangularly shaped shelves do not offer a great amount of actual storage space, so that a pair is a sound investment if two can be found similar enough in treatment and proportion to be called a pair.

Cherry has long been the collector's idea of a corner cupboard par excellence, and there is no denying that the mellow tone of fine old cherry is hard to surpass. More than that, where an ensemble in one particular wood is to be worked out, cherry, which was used in tables, stands, bureaus, chairs, and cupboards of all kinds, will usually most quickly and satisfyingly reward the searcher.

Corner cupboards were generally made in two sections, an upper and a lower, which are easily detachable—a fact which makes transportation a comparatively simple problem. The upper section may have either one or two glass doors, the number of panes varying, according to size, from six to twelve. Sometimes the upper row of panes is set off by an architectural turning of the upper part of the door frame, though often the design is very elementary. The lower, enclosed part of the cupboard may have either one or two doors. Here as elsewhere the amount of detail as to hinges, feet, or turning helps to determine the purchase price.

Corner cupboards, more than most pieces of Pennsylvania provenance, display evidences of very superior craftsmanship, to such an extent, in fact, that it may occasionally be necessary to turn down an article which by its very excellence would put the rest of the furniture of the room out of countenance. Since simplicity seems to be the keynote of the artistry of the Pennsylvania Dutch, more may be lost than gained by mixing highly refined pieces with those which are frankly of farmhouse character. Over-elaborate effects in pine or poplar, in particular, may well be too showy.

For instance, one cupboard which came up at auction not long ago had a broken arch top which would have been peculiarly effective in mahogany, but which in pine was extremely pretentious, with its accompaniment of acorn finials, carved rosettes, and reeded and scalloped molding. The single arched door was bordered with triple reeded molding, connecting half-turned rope-carved columns. These ornamental devices in themselves were not without beauty, but the total effect was one of conscious ostentation rather than of ornamental significance. More effective in every way was an equally early cupboard (both pieces probably were of about 1800) with its old blue paint essentially intact. This cupboard, also of pine, was in two parts; the upper had twin arch doors with a reeded keystone at the center; the lower, two drawers, paneled doors, and a molded base. Such a cupboard was far better suited to the display of treasures than its companion, which called attention to itself.

There is still another kind of cupboard suited to rooms furnished in simple pieces—the hanging corner cupboard. These were usually off-hand products, and were well conceived for their purpose of providing a small but convenient storage place for keys or articles which for one reason or another were best kept out of children's reach. They are found in various sizes. Some had two shelves large enough to accommodate the household supply of candles or oil lamps. Some had a shallow drawer or two in addition, either at the top or the bottom of the cupboard. Usually there was a single solid wooden door, which fastened with a wooden button, although now and then a specimen is found in which the shelves are un-protected by anything more substantial than a cut-out framework. Almost all of them, however, were cumbersome, with their inch-thick boards and unrelieved massiveness.

Lacking a cellar kitchen or enclosed porch in which to make immediate use of such a convenient object, modern householders still find it adaptable in various ways. The natural pine, when refinished, is an excellent back-ground for the display of a few pieces of pewter. Again, it may be used to house a collection of candlesticks or of colorful glass lamps, or, for that matter, any special treasures which demand an individual refuge.

As an adjunct to this convenient corner cupboard, the three-cornered framework with a cut-out circle at the top to accommodate a wash bowl can be recommended. As a matter of fact, this corner washstand still serves a useful purpose in an occasional summer place where plumbing arrange-ments are not of the most adequate. A colorful spatter pitcher and basin can be placed nowhere else quite so conveniently, and with a handy storage compartment below, a small drawer or two to hold toilet articles, and a hanging cupboard over all, the ensemble can achieve an air of positive dis-tinction. The principal difficulty in securing a satisfactory effect lies in the fact that the corner washstands seem usually to be less sturdy in construction than the suspended cupboards. Consequently an air of top-heaviness may result unless the buyer exercises caution in securing two pieces which mate well in size and construction. There seems to be good reason to suppose that a considerable majority of the cupboards were much earlier than the stands, and if the buyer feels that he must adhere to a highly restricted period he will probably have to abandon one article or the other.

Another primitive piece which is occasionally found on the market is the water or bucket bench, more likely to be serviceable than ornamental. Originally it was a simple cupboard or glorified bench intended for kitchen or porch use, with wooden doors below, a drawer or two, and an open top, suggestive of the Welsh cupboard, to which in a sense it is kin. Sometimes the top had cut-out holes, the diameter of which was gauged to provide a resting place for water buckets, and perhaps a wash basin. Other specimens show no such cut-out portions, the top of the closed section simply providing a shelf on which to set the pails, and in some cases the dish-washing para-phernalia. These pieces, generally listed as "antique sinks" at country auctions, are almost always of softwood and of rude construction, although a really usable bench is found often enough to make the search worth while. In superior examples the back has been built up to a distance of about twenty inches, and a row of short drawers placed at the top. Such pieces now serve very adequately as sideboards. Sometimes kitchen sinks closely approached the form of those used in the country only a generation or two ago, before there was "water in the house." The husband of the woman who carried water from the spring for household use apparently now and then took pity on his wife's benighted state, and did his best to make dish-washing seem more attractive by lining a portion of the top with zinc and providing a drain. Occasionally paneled doors and scalloped aprons added to the beauty of these pieces.

At a recent antique show an exceptionally well-proportioned bucket bench, with raised panels and simple, scalloped back, was offered for sale at a fantastically high price, this latter circumstance being occasioned by the fact that the piece had been "restored" and decorated in blue paint with an elaborate flower fancification. As a piece of furniture it was appealing, but as an antique it would have to be considered spurious, since evidence seems to be lacking that such decorations were ever used on this lowly piece of equipment. The case is not necessarily one of *caveat emptor*, since hand-painted furniture of whatever provenance has been steadily increasing in popularity; but if the owner wishes the real thing he will have to stick to the plain softwood bench until such time as incontrovertible evidence for the gaudier piece comes to light.

Spice cupboards, too, are to be found in Pennsylvania as well as in New England, their small compartments restricting or defining their usefulness to a great extent. The usual spice cabinet is merely a cupboard of small drawers, ranging in number from four to fifty, or even more. Larger specimens, which take on the aspect of furniture rather than mere accessories, usually rest squarely on the floor, and may have an open shelf or shelves at the top. When the original brass knobs are intact and the proportions are pleasing to the eye, they make a most desirable place for housing collections of such small objects as buttons, knives, forks and spoons, and cooky cutters. They seem not to have claimed the attention of collectors to any marked degree, at least until recently, and excellent specimens are thus still available.

Small hanging spice cabinets, with several tiers of drawers, either all of one size or of various gradations, may find a use in any room of the house, and in particular as a useful adjunct to the sewing room. Now and then a painted or stenciled one turns up, the decorations of which are similar to those on the Pennsylvania Dutch painted chairs. An object of that kind is a real find, and is worth making a sacrifice to acquire, even if no end further than that of beauty alone is to be served. Some sticks of cinnamon bark and a handful of cloves in the cabinet help to preserve the old-time atmosphere, and altogether the proud possessor will be more inclined to display it in the dining or living room than in the kitchen. A particularly good specimen is painted in dark brown, with a pert, conventionalized floral design in faded cerise and green on its four small drawer fronts. It has cherries on the sides and on the curved backing, which extends about six inches above the topmost drawer. The drawers, incidentally, are set one above the other, rather than in two tiers, as is customary.

Similar to the spice box is the salt box, another small cabinet, usually homely and unpretentious. These boxes, with their curved, elongated backs, were usually pierced with a hole to slip over the head of a nail. No more common to Pennsylvania than spice boxes, they are still sufficiently naïve to fit in with the simple furnishings of a Pennsylvania farmhouse kitchen.

Then there is the pie cupboard, the acquisition of which will cost the antique hunter a good many hours, if not days and weeks, of searching. This tin safe is a striking piece of furniture when one is lucky enough to find it in good condition. Its essential construction is that of a plain, one-piece, one- or two-door cupboard of stark architectural simplicity. It may be three feet in width and four or five in height, or even larger, its interior consisting merely of a number of removable shelves. Its charm lies in the pierced tin panels which cover its framework, doors and all. These panels repeat a simple design, a star, a bird, or a geometric motif, the perforations as a rule extending entirely through the tin. The doors may be composed of single panels each, although sometimes the sheets of tin are imposed on a wooden framework, the whole then taking on the aspect of a pine cupboard completely covered with tin patches. A good specimen at a country acution a few years back was rendered attractive by a neatly sawed out apron at the bottom and by tapering slipper feet. Another, at a different place, boasted of fifteen tin panels repeating a spread-eagle design, supplemented with ovals and diamond scrolls. Were the luscious pies of the Pennsylvania Dutch housewives set away to cool in these capacious repositories, their fragrance stealing through the pierced tin walls? There seems to be some reason for supposing so. Perhaps, too, as one dealer contends, they were used at one time for the storing of cuts of meat in the local butcher shop. Not inconceivably they may have served both purposes, and yet have been created originally for something entirely different. A further air of mystery is added by the fact that some of them were suspended in air by a rope from the ceiling, presumably to keep out preying rodents. When judiciously scoured and waxed to prevent rust, they are a fortunate acquisition for the person who has a taste for the unusual.

Finally there is the severely simple, broad, kitchen cupboard of pine, with two knife drawers, and with three full-length shelves enclosed by paneled wooden doors. A super-imposed "balcony" about four inches high kept articles from falling off the top of the cupboard at back and sides. As long as finer articles were plentiful, these humbler pieces were given scant attention, but within the past few years a good number have made a proud trek from the out-kitchen or cellar to the living or dining room.

Desks

L ET it be said once more that the antiques enthusiast, in his endeavor
to recapture the elusive atmosphere of bygone times, will sooner or later
have more atmosphere on his hands than he knows what to do with, unless
somewhere along the line he begins to exercise a Spartan restraint of the
acquisitive instinct. The collecting urge being what it is, the tendency is
to buy whatever strongly appeals to the buyer, and then, by a process of
rationalization, find a justification for its use in his home.

Take desks, for instance. The modern man or woman of affairs naturally
needs one or more. What, then, could be more logical than to look for a
Pennsylvania Dutch example to go with other Pennsylvania Dutch furniture?
And, further, what could be more natural than for dealers to have the *very*
thing? This is not for a moment to imply that there is anything wrong with
the person who needs a convenient place to dispatch his correspondence, or
with the dealer who can produce a desk when he knows that there will be
a market for it. However, consider the Pennsylvania Dutchman of yester-
year for a moment before setting out on a quest for the desk that once graced
the study of the old stone house in the limestone counties of southeastern
Pennsylvania.

First and foremost, the Dutchman was a farmer, a man whose chief
satisfaction was in the skillful cultivation of his soil. From dawn to dusk
he pursued his round of agrarian activities, six days out of the week. On the
seventh he refrained from physical labor, went to church, and caught up on
his social affairs. As for his wife, she had even less spare time than her
spouse, with her perennial cooking, cleaning, sewing, child-rearing, garden-
ing, and multitudinous chores of all kinds. Chairs and benches, cupboards
and tables, bureaus and beds were necessities, but just what useful purpose
would have been served in the average household by a desk of any kind?
The clock shelf and the parlor table held the almanac and the Bible, which
comprised the literary matter of the house except in unusual cases; and as
for the infinitesimal amount of correspondence that had to be carried on,
one end of the kitchen table was usually sufficient.

The Pennsylvania Dutch farmer was not a lettered man. In fact, he
often occupied the position of being almost a man without a written language.

The German tongue of his ancestors gradually disappeared in the English-speaking colony of Pennsylvania, even before the School Law of 1834 officially called for English instruction in all the public schools of the Commonwealth. As for English, he read it either badly or not at all, and had little occasion to speak it, since he seldom left the Dutchland for any reason. That left the South German dialect, which existed only as an oral language up until the nineteenth century, and did not meet with general favor in writing for years after that.

It is not hard to see, therefore, why the Dutchman, who read but little and wrote less, seems not to have produced the distinctive article of furniture which would so grace the study, den, or library of today's gentleman farmer. To be sure, there were the rural squires and justices of the peace, and the later generations who went out into the world and became eminent in many fields, but by that time the age of individual craftsmanship had all but passed, and importation of furniture had become a commonplace. Make no mistake: there are good Pennsylvania desks, Bachman desks, for example, but they generally came from the cities and the towns, from the schools and the stores rather than from the farmsteads. If the buyer wishes to secure one of them, rather than to follow the present-day trend and build one in when he sets about the inevitable remodeling to make up for the lack of sufficient closet space in nearly all old houses, he has a fair variety to choose from. Basically there are four types, although individual enterprise and interpretation provided such variations that there may seem to be several more.

First of all there is the "schoolmaster" desk, which once occupied a commanding position at the front of the rural schoolroom, especially when, as was frequently the case, it was mounted on a platform. There is a certain nostalgic appeal to the sentimental or to the imaginative person in this scarred relic of the far past, perhaps enough to atone for the fact that it is often much less utilitarian than picturesque.

In its most elementary form this desk was little more than a four-legged table, surmounted by a casual arrangement of pigeonholes. As such it would hardly appeal to the buyer unless it were of good solid walnut or cherry, with the legs neatly turned, and with enough actual writing surface to make it practical. One thing is of paramount importance, and that is the proper height of the writing surface from the floor. Unless the buyer is willing to imitate the early schoolmaster, and sit on a high stool at a high desk, he had better sacrifice picturesqueness for practicality. No one who has not actually tried it can imagine the acute discomfort that comes of making out checks or answering letters while perched atop a stool with legs a foot longer than normal. Perhaps the schoolmaster did not mind, or perhaps the stools of those years were more adaptable than are the ones of today. Perhaps, even, he stood up! In any event we shall probably not know, for the pedagogues are dead and gone, and with them seem to have vanished the stools to their desks. The nearest thing to a satisfactory substitute appears to be a tall bench evolved for the purpose by a well-known reproducer of early American furniture—a backless bench which offers little but absolute simplicity and a place to sit down.

Not all the schoolmaster desks are so proportioned, however, and there are enough pleasing variations from the norm of a mere table top equipped with pigeonholes to make the search worth while. A representative specimen would have two drawers at the front and be equipped with a "slope fall" top which when closed would conceal a central compartment flanked by pigeonholes and several small drawers. The lid when open would be supported by the table surface on which it rested or by two sliding boards at the side which could be pulled out of the wall of the desk for that purpose.

Refinements of this basic pattern are various. One is the narrow letter files which could be pushed in at the sides of the outermost pigeonhole compartments so that they were flush with the drawer and pigeonhole fronts. Another is the secret drawer, which most buyers are eager to believe is unique with their own finds. Actually, secret drawers are as like as peas in a pod, and are to be found in exactly the same place in all old desks of this type—at the back of the central well. The number of secret drawers customarily varies from one to four. Another variation which serves to give character to the schoolmaster desk is a pyramidal stacking of the small drawers, to conform to the slope of the lid when it is closed. These stacked drawers may have either plain or serpentine fronts, and now and then show very fine workmanship.

Purely as a matter of speculation, it is possible that the surviving finer examples of schoolmaster desks came from the homes of the schoolmasters rather than from the actual scenes of their scholastic labors. Yet when one remembers the itinerant nature and lack of prestige of the early run-of-the-mill country teacher, the whole thing remains but little more than speculation. In later years the teacher was more often a man of some consequence in his community, frequently taking in his stride such offices as justice of the peace, veterinarian, homeopathic physician or, even, preacher. A man of such importance would certainly need at least one desk at home to help him keep his affairs straight.

The second of the four fundamental types of desks is the bureau-desk, the lower part of which contains three or four drawers, the most capacious ordinarily being at the bottom. Such desks cannot really be thought of as typically Pennsylvania Dutch, since they are often to be found wherever antiques come to light. In general they are the most satisfactory type which can be secured, for they are of superior workmanship, offer a maximum of working and storage space, and harmonize well with most period furniture.

For the searcher who is doing his level best to seek out pieces of genuine Pennsylvania origin, about the only assurance that he can get is a reasonably authentic history of the piece he has under consideration. Lacking that, he must simply take his chances that his find was built in Pennsylvania rather than in Jersey or Maryland or Connecticut.

Bureau-desks are generally termed "slope-fall" or "slant-top" desks in the trade, and what has been said of pigeonholes, drawers, and secret compartments in the discussion of schoolmaster desks applies equally to them. Some of these pieces are beautifully inlaid with holly or other light wood, or even with mother-of-pearl. The brass drawer pulls, keyhole escutcheons, and other characteristics of early period furniture are to be found, and in later times the glass or wooden knobs associated with the Empire or Victorian styles. Once more the prospective purchaser will be compelled to consider his find carefully in the matter of height, or he may discover too late that the beautiful slope-fall top which was so loudly extolled by the auctioneer comes to rest uncomfortably under his armpits when let down as a writing surface. Obviously the sensible thing to do is to get a chair of convenient height and seat oneself at the dropped lid before the auction begins, in order to avoid disappointment. Lacking such an opportunity, the latecomer or the distant spectator may still have the somewhat negative satisfaction of reflecting that a four-drawer desk is almost always too tall, to say nothing of its being definitely too heavy!

There is another point to be considered, which is that these over-sized pieces of furniture may be used as chests of drawers, especially when they are structurally attractive. The desk top may be a convenient place to preserve and file papers and documents of all kinds, even though it is obviously a place at which one transacts his business while standing up. It is not inconceivable, for that matter, that so many of these breast-high lids exist because there was so little necessity, when life was simpler, for any great amount of writing to be done.

The favorite cabinet wood of rural Pennsylvania was cherry. Bureau-desks, though, were seldom constructed of one wood only, with the possible exception of walnut. A striking combination is cherry and curly maple, especially when the particular variant known as "tiger" or striped maple is employed. The maple is customarily used as a veneer on drawer fronts. One good specimen of the taller kind is of solid cherry, except for the veneer, and with an additional inlay of mahogany, so arranged as to give the maple the effect of paneling. The resultant combination of dull red, brown, and warm yellow is strikingly effective. This same desk has a two inch wide banding of mahogany just above the elaborate apron at the bottom, extending on around the sides to the rear feet.

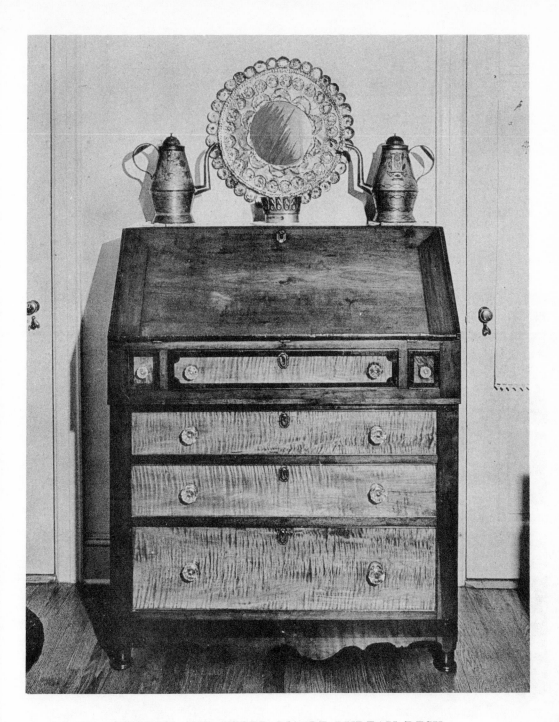

CHERRY AND TIGER MAPLE BUREAU DESK

PINE STOREKEEPER DESK

The third basic type of desk is the familiar tall secretary, with its drawers in the lower part and book shelves behind glazed or wooden doors in the upper. Frankly, there is little about any of these secretaries to mark them as being different from similar pieces to be found elsewhere in the country. Really good specimens seldom found a market outside of the larger centers of population, for one thing because there was so seldom a need anywhere else for such a thing as a secretary-bookcase. Occasionally a country-made specimen turns up, in cherry or walnut, but its design has so obviously been copied from that of standard patterns that the subject need not be discussed here.

Then there is the kneehole desk, which is also apt to be a rather superior piece of furniture; so much so that as a farmhouse relic it is at once suspect. Now and then there are authentic pieces, to be sure, as in the case of one dealer who has become so attached to a small-sized maple desk that he has placed a fantastically high price on it for fear someone might catch him in an unguarded moment and talk him into selling it. This desk has three serpentine drawers on either side of the central knee recess, and in its simple dignity would do credit to the house of anyone fortunate enough to secure it. Maple, incidentally, is much less common than mahogany in this particular type. The mere fact of its being maple at all led the present owner to trace it to its humble place of origin to verify its genuineness, since good kneehole desks are almost invariably the product of skilled cabinetmakers.

A variant of this type occurs in what is called, primarily because there has been at least one substantiating instance, the storekeeper desk. The wood of the particular specimen which has been chosen for mention is pine, with the exception of the two turned legs, which may be either maple or cherry. The kneehole recess is at one side rather than in the middle, the rest of the space under the flat top, with the exception of two drawers set side by side, being devoted to a large storage cabinet with a single wide door. This circumstance explains the curious fact of there being but two legs, the closed portion having four posts of its own. One drawer has its original lock, key, and escutcheon; the other was never intended to be locked. The top of the desk has an unbroken surface, and its twenty-six by fifty-six inch dimensions offer ample accommodation for telephone, typewriter, and the secretarial appurtenances that seem to accumulate on desks. The storage cupboard has a simple apron from post to post below the door. The back of the desk is of rough boards, so that it must necessarily be used flat against the wall. It was found in an old country store in Bucks County, and was sold with a full quota of old string, tags, and rubbish bearing mute evidence that many years had elapsed since it had known the touch of a cleaning day.

Another desk, much earlier, perhaps as early as 1750, is a crude but interesting type called by the dealer who discovered it a "lowboy kneehole desk," probably because of its size, since it in no way suggests the conventional lowboy. It is but thirty-six inches wide, and at first glance conveys the impression of a slope-fall desk top set upon a very simple bench. The ends of the desk, however, and what would be the sides of the bench, are constructed of a single plank apiece, cut back at the top to accommodate the lid at about a forty-five degree angle when it is closed. The back is of rough boards, and stops short of the floor by about two inches. The desk has two drawers, one above the other, the lower being the larger. The interior has two small scalloped pigeonholes and two small drawers, centered with an open scalloped pigeonhole and one long drawer. There are letter compartments at the end. This desk was sold in the rough, and because of its very evident age and rarity has probably since remained untouched.

This question of restoration, incidentally, is one which fortunately need concern the buyer of Pennsylvania Dutch antiques less than almost any other. The possessor of a Goddard break-front or of a Philadelphia lowboy would probably be unwise to tamper with any defect, for fear of placing a very considerable investment in jeopardy. But the person who has paid a modest sum for the rugged furniture of Pennsylvania Dutch provenance may proceed with a far greater feeling of comfort or ease, knowing that much less hinges on the result. Certainly ordinary pieces acquired in the rough should be cleaned up and put in usable condition if one is to live contentedly with them. If, however, there is a reasonable possibility that they will be offered for resale in a short time, better prices can be expected for articles that are patently in their original or untouched condition.

Tables

So popular is the cherry table among lovers of old wood that when a country sale in its interminable list of oddments includes one, the roadsides will be lined far and near with cars bearing out-of-state licenses. Any old Pennsylvania homestead being broken up and its household wares offered for sale is likely to have one such, provided that local dealers in antiques have not been able to make a "dicker" ahead of time and carry it away triumphantly. The cherry table, of course, is not always immediately recognizable as cherry, for the rigorous use to which it has been subjected in kitchen or cellar has sometimes destroyed its soft tones of red or brown, leaving an unattractive gray which to the uninitiated has neither charm nor desirability. Yet underneath the unprepossessing exterior the mellow old wood is ready to emerge with more than its pristine beauty when subtly handled by the expert.

Perhaps one reason why these tables can be bought outside the antiques establishments is that they have been in continuous use by their owners up to and even including the actual day of the sale, and dealers, therefore, have been turned down when they made their offers. More than once, as the collector passes through a living room or kitchen to inspect the offerings of the day, before the auctioneer has begun, he will find that a very good table has been loaded with crockery, kitchen utensils, or jar upon jar of canned fruit, all of which must be sold before the merits of the table itself can be appreciated. In any event a really good table would be withheld by the auctioneer as long as possible, for the sheer drama of the thing. Once the antiques have been sold, many of the crowd will disappear—both the city folk who have no interest in the more prosaic articles, and those of the frankly curious who have waited for no purpose other than to see how much things will "fetch." It is up to the auctioneer, therefore, in fairness to his employers (to say nothing of the size of his own commission) to keep the crowd together and good-natured as long as possible.

Undeniably, part of the satisfaction in owning a good cherry table, as any antique for that matter, comes from recalling the circumstances under which it was acquired. Possibly the gala air of the rural vendue is responsible for bidders going off the deep end; possibly, too, the firm determination of the local schoolmarm to keep the table "in the family" acts as a stimulus to an ultimately round price. Whatever the reason, one is not often able honestly to boast of a real bargain at a country sale. It is only on a rainy day or at a poorly publicized sale that worthwhile objects go for a song.

What is there about cherry tables that makes them the *ne plus ultra* of those who are furnishing in the country manner? For one thing, of course, there is the beauty of the wood itself, which is nowhere else so evident as in the broad expanse of table top and gleaming drop leaf. Then, too, the adaptability of the various sizes for dining tables or wall tables or for use in hall, study, or library makes them as sensible a buy as the most practical-minded could wish. Some have four legs, others six; the drop leaves may be (and usually are) rectangular, but may be half-moon shaped or scalloped or rounded at the corners. The legs are usually simply turned, but may be vertically or spirally reeded. Customarily there is but one drawer; infrequently a specimen with a drawer at each end comes to light. Almost always the construction is of solid cherry throughout, although now and then a striking combination of tiger maple and cherry is found.

The drop-leaf table is in many respects the most satisfying of the vast cherry family, but is by no means the only collectible form. Smaller tables, whether square or oblong, can be found in sizes and proportions which make them suitable for end tables, bedroom tables, and breakfast tables, as well as for the dozen casual uses occasioned by the problems of individual houses. Since there is such a variety available, there is little point in indicating more than a few of their most noticeable characteristics.

Most small cherry tables once served in a minor, ancillary capacity as "stands," and were intended merely to hold house plants, lamps, and other commonplace objects. For that reason, perhaps, they received a minimum of decorative treatment, happily for those who wish to make use of them now. An attractive feature sometimes found is a top with a beaded edge at the front. Another is a neat drawer front with an attractive brass pull instead of the more usual wooden or glass knob. Very effective, too, although far from common, are rope-turned legs, instead of the usual elementary turnings given to most table legs.

More elegant in effect are the small stands sometimes called sewing cabinets, with two or more drawers at the front, in a combination of curly maple and cherry, or mahogany and cherry, or even of all three woods. When the drawers are of the bow front type, the buyer is getting still more for his money. An unusually fine sewing table was put on the market only recently, when its owner found he had to reduce the size of his collection in order to move from a house into an apartment. The top and the drop leaves (these in themselves an unusual feature) were of solid cherry, the rest of the construction, including neatly turned legs with ornamental half columns, being in solid curly maple. The three drawers, instead of being shallow, were so generously proportioned that they extended to within a few inches of the floor. This unique little piece was twenty inches wide with the leaves down, and thirty inches high.

At least one necessity occasioned by the demands of modern living, however, cannot be found among the small cherry stands of yesterday, and that is the low coffee table. For the increasing number of people who feel that the shoemaker's bench fad has about run its course, and for those who find little attraction in marble-topped, iron-legged makeshifts or in adapted "reproductions," another alternative (possibly just as repugnant to the true antique lover!) is to secure an oblong cherry stand having the proper surface, and to cut down its legs to the desired height. It is a fairly simple operation to have the legs re-turned, for that matter, and if the householder can feel proud of, instead of apologetic for, such an achievement, one recurrent problem will have been solved. Since the value of the table as an antique will have been destroyed, it would be well to attempt such a process only with an inexpensive stand.

So much talk of cherry does not preclude the fact that tables essentially similar in style and construction were also made of other woods. This is especially true of the drop-leaf variety, of the size now so much sought after for dining tables. Most arresting of all, because so little imitated as yet, is the tiger maple table, the golden amber of which adds a rich tone to any room furnished in maple, pine, or cherry. For some reason which remains to be explained, these are sometimes found in larger sizes than similarly constructed ones of cherry, the drop leaves falling almost to the floor. Walnut drop leafs are also available, although they are less common, and perhaps less attractive, than the others. There seems to be an affinity between cherry or maple and old pewter or spatterware or Gaudy Dutch, not to mention blue milk glass, that does not exist with walnut.

Drop-leaf tables, of whatever wood, are by no means the only kind to go with a Pennsylvania Dutch setting and, in fact, are definitely not among the earliest known. For the admittedly primitive room there is the sawbuck tavern table, which is of good size, and which will double equally well for use as a dining or a library table. The top is rectangular in shape, often slightly under eight feet in length and about thirty inches in width, although naturally there are many variations. The legs, or more properly the X-leg supports, are connected by a straight center stretcher. Desirable elaborations are scalloped legs, drawers, or carving on any portion of the frame. The usual wood is pine, but specimens in walnut are not unknown.

Part and parcel with the tavern table is the kind known to the trade as the bench table. This usually has bracket feet, and sometimes has a closed lower compartment intended for the storage of linen. As is the case with some of the tavern tables, the top may be tilted back to stand vertically. The buyer who would make practical use of one of these is often faced with a major job of restoration, as the top is usually badly scarred, warped, or even splintered.   As it became possible to secure finer household pieces, the original owners discarded this crude furniture by a gradual process which included the cellar kitchen, the spring house, and perhaps the chicken coop. Needless to say, if it is used at all in modern homes it must be used judiciously.

Not so common is the very early Moravian Communion table, the dates for which seem to be in dispute among antique dealers.   The usual claim seems to be for about 1700 to 1725, but inasmuch as the Moravians did not settle in Pennsylvania much before 1741 the date would seem to call for a revision of about twenty-five years at least.   One good specimen of this kind, offered for sale at an auction a few years back, measured fifty-seven by thirty-two inches at the top.   Its fine, turned legs were connected by flat outside stretchers, pegged together.   Other attractive features were a drawer, a scalloped apron, arched ends, and a shelf.   While one would hesitate to call it Jacobean, its somewhat massive construction and the turning of the legs would indicate that its maker probably had some acquaintance with the furniture, at least the ecclesiastical furniture, of that time.   The top, of softwood, showed that it had had hard usage.

Among other early tables, not yet so scarce that the anxious buyer need feel that he is on the trail of an almost inaccessible museum piece, is the gateleg variety.   However, so much has been said of this form in other works that there seems to be little point in repeating it here.   Gatelegs are among the articles of furniture which seem to have found a wide circulation among all the Colonies, and could hardly lay claim to Pennsylvania Dutch origin, even when a given example of attested Pennsylvania provenance comes to light.

The same thing is probably true of the slipper-footed hutch table, with its removable top, open compartment, and straight sides.   Yet so little attention has this compact specimen received that its owner will not usually be called upon to defend it in the face of those who insist that there is nothing particularly Pennsylvanian in either hutch tables or gatelegs.   The hutch table is not of the kind that called for an expert knowledge of cabinetmaking, but is quite at home with painted furniture and other manifestations of Pennsylvania Dutch decoration.   A typical specimen is of softwood and has a top spread of about thirty by thirty-seven inches.   An unflattering commentary on this type of early table is that it is no more than a flat top placed on a box open at one side and set on end.   If the statement is qualified by saying that the box has four substantial posts serving as legs, and that the top fits on it very snugly by means of cleats, the characterization is essentially true, albeit somewhat bluntly put.

Representative of the Dutchland is the dough-box or stretcher dough table, which has both oddness and utility to recommend it. In days gone by, the housewife, for whom bread baking was at least a semi-weekly task, used this slant-sided box, perhaps thirty-six inches long and eighteen wide, to mix her dough and get it ready for baking. Mounted on its simple stretcher base, it was light enough in weight to be moved easily from one spot to another. Nowadays, with its top lid in position, it makes a very convenient storage place for magazines, or offers an equally accessible refuge for patterns or for unfinished sewing. Not much publicity has been given to the dough box, so that it is possible to secure good specimens without too much trouble.

Still other small tables and stands are come upon without an inordinate amount of searching, from the very simplest of farm-made square walnut stands with a single drawer and square-tapered legs to excellent stretcher stands with removable tops, balustered legs, and Chippendale brasses. The sad facts are that most of these have had new tops added at some late date, that the addition of casters has cracked the legs, or that the drawer fronts have had very rough treatment. The thing which makes them more desirable, even in the face of repairs that will have to be undertaken, than the Victorian pieces which clutter up so many country shops, is their utter absence of weird scroll-work and unstable architectural gimcrackery. They were made to be used rather than to be looked at, but when refinished are well worth looking at, too.

Concluding the list of tables which the householder may want, there is the varied array of little round-topped fellows which go so well near the fireplace or before windows. Like other pieces not peculiarly Pennsylvania Dutch, they are not infrequently found in the Dutch country, and choice specimens have often been pictured and described in furniture books. Tilt-top tables, bird-cage pedestals, pie-crust edges, snake feet—they are too well known to call for any particular description here.

Beds and Coverlets

MORE than a few persons, scanning the old rope beds which served our fore-bears, decide somewhat hastily that in respect to sleeping they will sacrifice old-time atmosphere to modern comfort. Perhaps, tempted by some par-ticularly appealing pineapple post or spool top, they yield a point, and de-cide to try just one for the guest room—but in that one act of yielding they are saved, for they will discover that with a modicum of common sense they can eat their cake and have it too. In other words, it is quite possible to have an old farmhouse bed, once accoutred with roping and a straw tick, and sleep comfortably upon it.

Here, as in choosing any furniture, it is largely a question of securing what will be in keeping with the rest of the typical Pennsylvania Dutch furniture. Gorgeous canopies above slender Sheraton posts are usually out of the question, no matter how charming they may be in interiors designed to accommodate them. Similarly, twin beds are out of the picture as such, for they did not exist in the days when *fractur-schriften* (illuminated writings) adorned the bedroom walls. However, there is a satisfactory compromise in the narrow three-quarter size bed, two of which may be placed in a large room without overcrowding. The problem of getting two just alike is not insurmountable if one is willing to stick to the simpler designs.

A story is told of a wealthy woman who was furnishing her summer "cottage" at one of the more luxurious summer resorts a few years back. She was able to supply many of her wants at the local antique shops, and, since money was no object, made considerable progress in a short time. Then arose the matter of twin beds and, try as she might, she could unearth none. Finally a helpful dealer said that if she would give him two weeks' time he could get her a pair, but that, owing to their exceeding rarity, they would cost three hundred dollars. The woman, who had practically given up hope, was delighted. So was the dealer, who took two very ordinary cherry beds of the usual size to a superior workman to cut down and "an-tique" them. The fraud went undetected. More than one country shop stocks "twin" beds which have been manufactured in the same way, and if the novice is content after having been told that the wood is genuinely old, or when an ancient and honorable pedigree has been displayed, he must pay the price for his naïveté or charge it up to experience.

Whatever its design, the Dutchman's bed was short, as befitted the countryman who, oftener than not, was noted for his girth rather than his height. As he said, "*Kurz und dick ist etwas auch*"—"short and thick is something, too." More than that, the bed was so high above the floor that the modern householder is filled with dismay at the prospect of having to use a stepladder to mount to the top of the springs and mattress to find a place of repose. There was a reason for that, too, for where could the trundle bed be better accommodated than under the tall one?

Still, the chances are that nowadays a six-footer may be planning to sleep in the Dutchman's bed—a six-footer whose family is probably not so large as to call for the offices of the trundle bed. The double problem of length and height can be solved at one time by substituting side boards for the old circular rails, attaching them lower down on the corner posts with angle irons. The boards may be cut to any length desired, keeping in mind the standard size of mattresses and springs, and finished to harmonize with the rest of the bed. These boards, of course, are invisible when the bed is dressed, and the entire operation is a very simple one. The old rails may be retained, and the value of the bed as an antique is in no way jeopardized.

Beds may be had in any of the woods used for other Pennsylvania Dutch furniture, with cherry and maple ranking as favorites. Softwood beds of pine or poplar are common, and walnut is also very often available. In fact, there are so many beds to be found that it is quite evident that until recently they were not regarded with too great favor by the antiquing fraternity, probably because the finer four-poster bedsteads, and field beds, were receiving so much attention.

The usual Pennsylvania Dutch bedstead, like other provincial Pennsylvania furniture, shows a marked degree of individuality in design, but at the same time manifests a certain kinship with the essentially massive pieces of the Empire period. The buyer should therefore consider his tentative acquisition rather thoughtfully, since the head- and footboards which lean so compactly against the wall in the shop sometimes takes on Gargantuan aspects when separated by an expanse of bedspread at home. One of the safe designs is that of the low post (so called to differentiate them from the "poster" or four-poster type) beds having simple turnings, terminating in a ball at the top. Refinements of this global decorative device are the steeple, the pineapple, and the acorn. Sometimes head- and footboards are identical, but frequently the headboard is taller and larger. One typical solid cherry bed, for instance, has a turned rail, decreasing in thickness from the middle toward the ends, set into the globes at the top of the head posts. Below this is a scalloped, cut-out panel in a single piece fitted into the posts farther down. The foot has a much smaller panel, with the rail joining the posts a few inches below the globe finials. The markings of the cherry posts are particularly attractive in this specimen. An essentially similar bed in maple almost black with age has two turned rails at the foot instead of a rail and a board, a common condition in low post beds.

The spool bed is one which is particularly suitable for the farmhouse or for the apartment because of its simplicity and its range of sizes. Spool or knob turning, whether in head or foot pieces or in the posts, gives an effect of lightness lacking in other forms, especially when, as is often the case, a light-colored wood like maple is used. An attractive feature is the arched headboard found on some beds. A later form suggests the Windsor style, with its slender vase- or spool-turned uprights and ring-turned legs. Many variants, of course, are to be found.

For rooms that will take very heavy furniture there is the sleigh bed, so called because of its resemblance to the sleigh that was once the principal conveyance on country roads in the winter. The solid headboard slopes backward at the top in rather a graceful curve, while the footboard may curve either inward or outward. Usually fine woods were employed for such beds, and considerable skill was used in their execution. Solid, standing close to the floor, they dominate any room in which they are placed.

Trundle beds have a place in the economy of many a summer home, admittedly not for their beauty, but rather for their utility and movability. In construction they are very simple, being no more than a small, solid frame on which a mattress can be placed. Once upon a time the trundle bed regularly accommodated the youngsters of the household, and in an emergency can be counted on again.

So rare that it is all but a myth is the painted bedstead in the tradition of the decorated chairs, and dower chests. Few such beds have come to the attention of collectors, although at least one Mennonite bed, so called, with an attractively stenciled headboard has been on the market very recently. A simple bedstead, painted in soft old blue and decorated with floral sprays, human figures, and an inscription in German, was offered a year or two ago by a dealer in fine Pennsylvania Dutch things, with the opinion that it might be Pennsylvanian. The asking price did not preclude the possibility! In form and feeling it closely resembled some of the similarly painted pieces that in recent years have been imported from Switzerland.

Lacking authority and fuller information in an admittedly baffling field, the searcher for a genuine painted bed would do well to pay a visit to the New York shop of an importer of old Swiss and French Provincial furniture. Here he will find excellent peasant artistry, utilizing many of the motifs that are commonly associated with the Pennsylvania Dutch. Such a condition is not at all strange, considering the fact that both the Swiss and the French Huguenots contributed extensively to Colonial settlements along the Atlantic seaboard. The conclusion that will be drawn, whether rightly or wrongly, is that seemingly unique pieces which do not fit into the by now well-established Pennsylvania Dutch category are very likely of European origin. They may be just as attractive, and may harmonize amazingly well with the primitive art forms of Pennsylvania, but as authentic native furniture they are suspect.

Incidentally, should the urge to acquire the old Swiss furniture become strong, the novice will do well to make a thorough investigation of each piece. For one thing, while the old paint and the old decorations and the old wood are probably genuine, the chances are at least fifty-fifty that the present object has been re-assembled out of the component parts of an entirely different piece of furniture. The great cupboards and other objects which have no exact American counterpart have been cleverly reduced to smaller cupboards, cabinets, and tables for the benefit of those Americans who long for the crude and primitive artistry of times gone by, no matter how attained. No particular blame attaches to the sellers, since they are usually quite frank about the matter when questioned.

Dressing a bed in Pennsylvania Dutch style is rather simpler than the tyro might feel, unless he is considering a four-poster. The old quilts and coverlets available today are often in surprisingly good shape, for they have almost invariably had the best of care and have seen but little service. Those which were actually used were worn out long ago, but those which were highly cherished, and therefore packed away in blanket chests, are frequently almost as bright as when they were new. They should be treated with respect, of course, for even the strongest of them demands considerate handling.

Coverlets fall generally into two classes, those which were woven and those which were created out of patches—and the infinite patience and ingenuity of their makers. The woven ones are usually the older and also the more serviceable of the two, because of the almost indestructible linen threads used in their weaving.

The making of woven coverlets goes back at least to Revolutionary times, and probably considerably farther. In the infancy of this particular handicraft, cumbersome looms were used, and only a narrow strip could be woven at one time with the result that most really old coverlets are composed of two parts sewed together. Since books have been written on the subject of coverlet designs, there seems to be no point in an extensive listing of them here, particularly as many of the finest pieces cost so much that they are out of the range of all except a very few collectors.

Designs embodying patriotic symbols are always desirable, especially those which utilize the eagle and those which reflect political campaigns of long ago. Tree forms are a frequent motif, and flowers are still more common. Purely geometric patterns, some of great intricacy, are to be found in the oldest specimens and in some quantity.   It is interesting that all the designs are built up of tiny angles because of the limitations of the hand loom, which could produce only straight lines.

Most coverlets were woven of wool and linen, the wool for warmth and the linen for durability.   The woolen fringe which frequently embellishes three sides of the coverlet (no fringe wasted on the end to be tucked in at the foot!) is usually quite badly worn, a factor which need not greatly concern the buyer.   Not all coverlets were dated, but naturally those which bear the year of their making are considered more desirable and command a higher price.   The customary procedure was to set the name of the owner, the year, and the name of the weaver into a good-sized square at one or more corners of the coverlet.   Sometimes this information, together with a patriotic slogan, was woven along the edges.

Undated coverlets should by no means be passed up if there are evidences of authenticity other than the date.   Most coverlets offered for sale as genuine really are genuine, although once in a while a reproduction, still *smelling* like new yard goods, finds its way into a shop or an antique show.   On the basis of the evidence at hand it would be out of the question to say how late the production of these coverlets continued, but dates in the 1830's seem to be most frequent.   Comparatively few dated specimens are found after that, perhaps because the hand looms went out of operation shortly after machine production became possible.   Many, perhaps most, of the very earliest specimens are undated.

Blue and white is probably the most pleasing color combination.   Judging by the number of blue and white coverlets in existence, it has always been a favorite.   Other colors occur, however, often in very harmonious combinations.   Red, green, and white, the white deepened by age to cream, is probably the commonest of these.   Occasionally the alchemy of time has produced an interesting tonal effect never contemplated by the weaver, as when the red has turned to brown and the green to a kind of mustard yellow. White alone did not come into favor until almost contemporary times.

So sought after by many persons are these old coverlets that in cases where only a fragment is available it is made into a pillow top, a chair seat, or a small table cover.   Nevertheless the buyer should not be deluded into regarding coverlets as extremely scarce, for many good ones are still available. Now and then purchasers secure badly moth-eaten ones, feeling that they had better take what they can get.   Perhaps they are right, but a little more shopping around might eventually result in greater satisfaction.

Patch quilts, like rag carpets, came from the overflow of materials used in homemade wearing apparel.   Unlike carpets, though, they were always made of new materials.   Considerable trading among neighbors was often indulged in, in order to secure a satisfactory variety of colors and patterns, but quilt block centers in small-figured red and yellow patterns were usually "store-bought." Indeed, certain red and yellow calico bolts in the old country stores appear to have been used for little else.

The number of quilt designs to be found is almost infinite, beginning with the simplest of "crazy-quilt" patterns, and culminating, perhaps, in those elaborate works of art in which each block is a little gem of the finest appliqué work. The smallness of the stitches and the intricacy of the quilting designs in these are proverbial. Needless to say, the value of the quilt is largely determined by the amount of hand work that has been done upon it. Tulips, so beloved by the Pennsylvania Dutch that they appeared in almost every possible phase of home decoration, make their appearance now and then on quilts, but not so often as the collector who is trying to find a good example might wish.

Since comparatively few patchwork quilts were dated, usually only those which were "friendship" quilts (in which individual blocks were contributed by friends) it is difficult to ascertain anything like their definite age. However, workmanship and design are much more to the point here than age. In fact, many antique lovers definitely prefer their patch quilts to be new, so that they may choose their own color combinations or patterns.

Old-time patch quilts were short, to fit the short beds of the times, sometimes too short for modern beds. One way out of the difficulty is to do as our Victorian grandmothers did in like circumstances: tuck the quilt in lightly at the foot, and then use a set of pillow shams to cover the pillows, preferably a pair with morning-glories, cherub faces, or "Good Night" and "Good Morning" neatly outlined in red. Those same Victorian grandmothers would not have exposed their patch quilts to the naked eye, however, but would have covered them neatly with a heavy, white woven spread. These spreads may still be found and, while not old enough to be rated as antique, are of sufficient age to give an old-time air to beds.

Of questionable antiquity but of admitted charm is the crocheted or knitted bedspread, which often lends the final touch necessary in turning an ordinary-looking room into a dainty, cheerful one. And, for those who cannot endure the thought of anything so modern as crocheting, there is some comfort in the reflection that every handmade spread is an heirloom in the making.

Chests

WHEN it comes to finding storage places for clothing, linens, and the hundred small necessities of everyday living, the collector has a fertile field among the survivals of bygone times.   If one could have a single wish granted, and if that wish were for the most desirable Pennsylvania Dutch chest, the Mahontongo Valley painted bureau would be the thing to ask for.   Since the furniture of this valley has been described earlier, it is necessary here to say no more than that only a few of these bureaus have ever come to light, but that these few are fully as attractive as their kindred cupboards.   As late as 1937 a commercial antiques auction listed one "with four graded drawers; upper drawer with jar of tulips, rose and daisy spray decoration; the other drawers painted red; colors, black, yellow and green; turned leg supports; solid ends."

The best Mahontongo Valley work surpasses this colorful array, utilizing birds, angels, and flowers in an arrangement which may possibly indicate some hidden spiritual significance.   Admittedly, there is not much point in dwelling upon the charms of this particular furniture, for there is so little of it that it is all but unobtainable, and the pickers and dealers lucky enough to spot a piece of it usually have immediate sale for it among their wealthy clients.   Still, it is pleasant to know that the possibility exists.   A less savory phase of the matter is that certain dealers have a tendency to describe as a Mahontongo Valley piece any Dutch article to which paint has been applied imaginatively, apparently counting on the wizardry of the name to help secure a sale.

After the painted bureau, the great *kas* is probably the most important storage piece to be found.   The *kas*, or cupboard, is usually of mammoth proportions, sometimes being more than six feet high and wide, and almost two feet deep.   It has two doors, in the manner of the tall Victorian wardrobes of not-too-happy memory, and is often mounted on turnip feet.   A very heavy architectural molding customarily graces the top.   While the *kas* is overpowering in any save a large room, it has great charm and distinction, whether stenciled in the patterns of the old chairs and rockers, or simply painted in colorful hues.

These articles are most often to be found in softwood, but at least one magnificent specimen in walnut has been on the market in the last year.

To be sure, it dwarfed the pleasant little room in which its owner had placed it, but its fine cabinetwork set it apart from the rank and file of such chests. Perhaps unique is the corner *kas* painted in madder red, owned by a Pennsylvania dealer. This little gem takes up no more space than a corner cupboard, which it somewhat resembles, and offers one happy solution to the problem of the closetless rooms of old houses.

Existing in greater numbers than is commonly supposed are the chests of drawers which are variously catalogued as bureaus, bureau high-chests, or bureau low-chests. Attractive pieces which will fit into a Pennsylvania Dutch setting are easily come upon, and offer no particular problem, so long as the buyer knows what he needs or wants. Chests of this kind are most popular in the four-drawer size, in cherry or pine. One indication of age, other than the condition of the wood itself, is in the ends which, in the earlier specimens, are of solid construction. In pine the most attractive feature of bureau chests lies in their sturdy, unassuming simplicity. In cherry, however, a favorite way of embellishing the chest was by a drawer-front veneer of cherry burl. Such burled fronts, infrequently of mahogany or walnut instead of cherry, add to the beauty as well as to the selling price of the article.

Drawers of these chests are sometimes all of the same height, but are more frequently graded, with the largest one at the bottom. The graded drawers seem to be the more highly regarded among collectors. After the drawers, another detail which is of interest is the feet; these, however, exist in many varieties, no one of which can be called distinctively Pennsylvania Dutch. Ogee and bracket feet are safe choices. Very early or very fine chests may have brass pulls or knobs, but knobs of glass or of wood stained to match the chest itself are in the majority. Now and then exceptional specimens show reeding on corner posts, or other decorative attempts on the part of some unusually skilled artisan with an eye for effect, but in general Pennsylvania chests are quite plain.

The Empire period contributed largely to the stock of bureaus remaining in the hands of dealers at present, and rare is the country auction which does not produce at least one such old-timer. If the home owner feels that he can safely introduce these rather bulbous, bulky articles into his home, he has the satisfaction of knowing that they are usually cherry, are easily refinished and look much neater after their encrustation of old paint has been removed. While they may hardly be called "finds," they are certainly useful, and will recede comfortably into the background in the face of more colorful—and more expensive—articles.

On the more spectacular side are the chests of drawers, usually rather small, of cherry and bird's-eye maple. This combination of dull red and honey amber was definitely intended to be "for pretty," and good workmanship was lavished on such pieces, which include stands, sewing tables, desks, and other articles as well.   The tall desks, incidentally, which are too high to use comfortably for their original purpose, are excellent as chests of drawers in bedrooms or as occasional pieces wherever a storage place is called for. The small compartments and drawers of the desk top are most convenient for depositing numerous small objects or collections, to say nothing of the satisfaction one may take in using the secret drawers for jewelry.   A roomful of this beautiful wood combination might be overwhelming unless very quiet draperies and carpets were chosen and a Spartan taste in accessories employed; but one well-proportioned piece makes a very effective accent in practically any room.

For the person who is looking for something quite out of the ordinary there is the tall linen press, a handy chest of drawers with a compartment above, containing several shelves concealed by wooden doors.   A representative early specimen has the upper part constructed of solid curly maple, surmounted by a scroll and urn finial.   There are three shelves enclosed by two paneled doors fitted with a tear-drop brass catch.   The lower section is in cherry, and contains four graded drawers, above the topmost one of which there is a curly maple panel.   The ends are solid, and a curved apron separates the French feet.   The corner posts are chamfered.

Finer in construction than other chests are the very tall pieces known variously as chest-on-frame, high-daddy, or simply high chests.   These customarily approach the better-known period furniture in design and execution, and call for little comment here.   Perhaps the high-daddy has the greatest claim to inclusion in the Pennsylvania Dutch home, not so much because it is in keeping with other rural furniture as because it just happened to be used in many houses, probably because it had been admired elsewhere. A typical walnut chest of this type has a short frame with scalloped apron, cabriole legs, and ball and claw feet.   Above this rise the tiers of graded drawers, five extending the full width of the chest, and then two short ones, surmounted by a topmost rank of three still smaller ones.   A pair of steps is needed in order to gain access to the upper compartments.

Most beautiful among all the Pennsylvania Dutch household effects is the blanket or dower chest, which has received a great deal of attention in recent years because of the revival of interest in folk art and articles.   Akin to the contemporary cedar chest, this low piece of furniture is among the oldest of the articles the collector of average means is able to secure.   That so many chests have survived, albeit in scarred and battered condition, is owing to the amazingly solid construction which has kept them in continuous service since the earliest days of the Colony.

These dower chests were the first hope chests, serving to hold the stores of linen which every well-brought-up country maiden began to make for

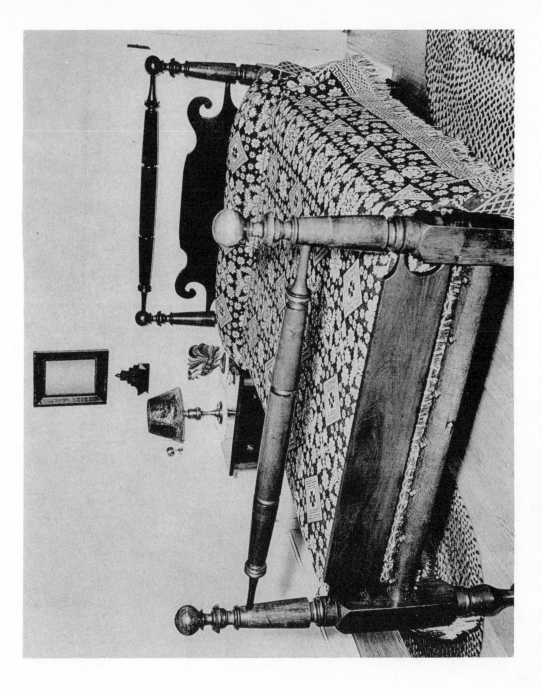

CHERRY BED: BLUE AND WHITE COVERLET

DUTCH FLORAL MOTIFS

herself almost as soon as she was able to hold a needle. Because of the romantic nature of the enterprise, and also because they offered an ideal surface for decoration, the chests were beautified with the various typically Pennsylvania Dutch motifs. According to tradition, some of the Dutchland counties are said to have developed their own peculiar ornamentation, with the result that chests are sometimes identified as of Berks or Lebanon or Lehigh provenance. Since most of the motifs can be traced back to European origins, however, it will take more evidence than is now at hand to enable anyone to state positively that a certain chest comes from Lebanon County, for instance, just because it bears certain decorative devices.

The favorite background color seems to have been a soft, rich blue, applied to top, ends, and front. Over this were painted the vases of flowers, the tulips and daisies, the stars, the birds, angels, unicorns, and other devices, usually but not necessarily within panels either painted or structurally created. The front of the chest, of course, received the more important decorations, but the ends and less frequently the top also came in for attention.

Many chests bear the name of the owner boldly lettered in the panels, with the accompanying date spaced widely across the front. Once in a while a signed specimen comes to light, but most of these have long since gone to the museums. It is generally conceded that one Christian Seltzer made the finest dower chests, and the term "Seltzer Chest" is synonymous with quality. The owners' names, appearing as they do in German lettering, sometimes confuse the amateur, particularly if he is not familiar with the German feminine ending "*in*," which is added to family names. A name like Anna Reber would thus appear "Anna Reberin."

In recent years the finest dower chests have become very rare, and are often held at fantastic prices. This condition has created a search for less perfect pieces, those which at an earlier time had been passed by as not good enough. Consequently it is sometimes possible to secure good chests with feet or base missing, or with the paint badly worn, at reasonable prices. It is simply a question of how badly the householder wants a dower chest. Several years ago an enterprising dealer who was also something of an artist secured a quantity of very old chests which had never been decorated and imitated the colorings and designs of well-known museum pieces with a reasonable degree of success. These were all signed by the artist, and were sold frankly as reproductions, so that there has never been any question of their being spurious. Since the death of their creator a few years ago they have risen in value.

Fully as attractive in their way as the more colorful, softwood chests are those of undecorated solid walnut, and less commonly of maple. The strap iron hinges, the great locks which operate with a massive key, the interior end compartment with the ingeniously concealed secret drawers, and the bracket or turnip feet are common to blanket chests of whatever kind. These chests will fit into the decorative scheme of every room in the house, whether kitchen, dining room, living room, or bedroom. They are as adaptable for storing records or sheet music in the music room as for packing away linens or china after a summer's use. One fine specimen of about 1800 or a little later stands about two feet high, its rich walnut apparently all the finer for the years it had been buried under coats of gray paint. The two small drawers at the bottom have the original brass pulls, and the old handmade lock and key are intact. It is still air-tight after more than a century of use. With its graceful bracket feet and simple lines it would be as much at home in almost any decorative scheme as it is in its present place in a Pennsylvania Dutch bedroom.

Equally serviceable, though not often so attractive, are unpainted blanket chests of pine, many of which have stood the rigors of time with less conspicuous success. The buyer of these will do well to take thought before investing any great amount of money in them, for unless they are particularly well made they will add little to the beauty of a room. Mediocre specimens have an unfortunate tendency to look more like a packing case than anything else.

Just as is the case of other pieces of furniture, oddities make their appearance now and then among chests. Without previous experience or expert advice the beginner will have to trust to his intuition when a meal chest gaudily decorated twenty years ago makes its debut as a "dower" chest. Now and then a sugar bin from Kentucky or a sea chest will come under the auctioneer's hammer. There is rather more than a grain of comfort, however, in the reflection that by this time there seem to be no unyielded-up secrets in Pennsylvania Dutch furniture. The gaudy newcomer is probably an impostor.

Floor Coverings

WHAT is placed on the floors of the Pennsylvania Dutch house will depend on several factors, notably the nature of the furniture, the flooring, and the amount of wear it will receive. Some of the authentic coverings are very colorful. Others are quite fragile, more for show than for service. The chances are that genuinely old coverings will be in the minority.

To begin with, where painted furniture is used, no floor covering should be of so dominant a brightness that the furniture will seem dingy or faded by contrast. Conversely, plain pine, and even cherry or walnut, often gains in interest from the strong hues of floor coverings. Since in most rooms the old floors with their wide boards will have been retained, square nail heads and all, and sanded and given a soft, lustrous finish it would be ill-advised to use too commonplace a covering or one that would conceal any considerable part of the surface, for a well-finished old floor can be a major part of the attractiveness of a room. Common sense will indicate, of course, that any floor covering of respectable years must be treated with consideration if it is to continue to give pleasure for a further period of time.

Distinctive among the possibilities are braided rugs, round or oval, which range in size from small ones of twenty inches or less in diameter to those which cover almost the entire floor space of the room. Rug braiding is an art in itself, and unfortunately one which is no longer much practiced. Fundamentally the process consists in starting with three strips of woolen or cotton (but never mixed) fabric and braiding them together with the rough edges carefully turned under. The strips have to be sewed together to provide a continuous length of braid, which is laid down circularly or in an oval pattern and each succeeding strand attached to the preceding one by stout linen thread. The art comes in getting a finished product that will show no rough edges and that, more important still, will lie flat on the floor. In the very large sizes it is almost always necessary to provide a rug-cushion anchor in order to avoid accidents. Of course, if one is satisfied with the machine-made products now obtainable in stores, all of this trouble will be eliminated.

The merits of the homemade rugs are evident at once, since they can be made in any size desired, and with exactly the colors needed for any given room.   Those who make their own seldom use new materials, but depend principally upon discarded garments, blankets, and the like, and the dye pot.   No rule as to the amount of material required for a rug can be given except the one current in rural Pennsylvania: "It takes a whole lot more than you think."   Either cotton or woollen materials can be used, but brighter and fuller-toned effects can be obtained in woollens.

Although hooked rugs seem to have enjoyed less favor in Pennsylvania than in New England they are commonly found.   Like the braided variety they were often made from discarded garments of silk, cotton, and other fabrics.   Consequently, those which may be picked up at the antique shops should be handled carefully and placed in rooms where they will not see extremely hard service.   Even new ones are not always entirely satisfactory, since they will not stand very vigorous cleaning, or remain bright for any great length of time.   Their beauty is such, however, that many people are willing to overlook their lack of durability.   Quite excellent Chinese hooked rugs of yarn have solved the problem for those who are not sticklers for the genuine Pennsylvania article.   In fact, they are often the only ones obtainable in larger sizes.   Canada has also been a fruitful source of supply, and tourists have been able to purchase good rugs quite reasonably.

Related to the braided and hooked floor coverings are the crocheted ones, the creation of which also calls for a particular kind of skill which comes from long practice.   These require less time in the making and, while often not so finely detailed in the finished form, are both attractive and serviceable. The smaller sizes are the more popular.

Other old-time rugs which were created out of odds and ends, "piece-patches," and the ingenuity of the housewife are still to be found in the best parlors of an occasional farmhouse.   One of these is the rectangular rug created by unraveling a few inches of small oblongs of knitted sweater, sock or mitten, and then sewing the portions still intact to a strong burlap back, somewhat like the overlapping of shingles on a roof.   The crinkled yarn, in its mellowed colors, thus makes a deep, warm, woolly rug particularly effective before a fireplace.   Other rugs also employ this overlapping device, some using long, narrow strips of many colors, and others petal-shaped patches, each blanketstitched to prevent fraying.   Yet another small rug which has enjoyed perennial popularity, and which has surprising durability, is the husk door mat.   Too stiff and immobile for most rooms, it finds its place on the terrace, covered porch, or even in the kitchen.

Pennsylvania also has a variety of distinctive carpeting to offer the seeker after a covering for floor areas of considerable size.   Most of these are "rag" carpetings, with the various effects which lend them character achieved by colored warp threads.   Rag carpeting was woven (and still is woven on many country looms) in various widths, with twenty-seven or thirty-six inches most common.   In earlier times, when random-width flooring was less prized than it is at present, the carpeting was sewed together and bound at the ends, and tightly stretched from wall to wall.   Before it was tacked down, a turkey feather dipped in turpentine was carefully applied to the base of the mop board, with the idea of discouraging moths.   This treatment was repeated each time the carpet was taken up for spring and fall house cleaning.

Over this carpet scatter rugs of the various "fancy" kinds, or simply of short strips of contrasting carpeting, were laid.   If carpeting was used, the ends were raveled out for an inch or more and the warp ends knotted at regular intervals to create a fringe.   Short woven rugs were common.

One practice in current usage is to sew the carpeting together but, instead of covering the entire floor, to create a "rug" of any desired size.   Another is to lay down single strips wherever fancy dictates.   Experience will soon teach that rag carpeting of whatever kind does not mix particularly well with hooked or braided rugs, but should be kept by itself for best effect. After all, it was a very prosaic commodity, evolved from the double desire for a floor covering and a way to utilize an accumulation of cast-off garments. As such it was an essentially homely thing, and without any great pretension to quality or prestige.

Plain carpeting frequently gave way to more elaborate effects when the rags, instead of being sewed together in hit-or-miss fashion for the loom, were sorted for colors, and enough red or blue, for instance, was sewed together at one time to create any desired width, often an inch, in the finished product. Thus, when the carpet was woven, a checkered effect could be achieved by alternating the colors of the warp at a like distance.   In most cases warp of one color, commonly black or brown, was used except near the edges, where combinations of various hues made bright strips running the full length of the carpet.   To achieve anything like a regular effect in the rags themselves it was necessary to do considerable dyeing, and before the days of the commercial products dyes of strong colors and great permanence and fastness were obtained from butternut or hemlock bark, madder, indigo, and various other sources.

Cutting and sewing carpet rags and winding them on balls was a steady winter evening occupation in many a rural home, whether or not there was any immediate need for carpeting.   Sometimes at country sales or in old attics carpet-rag balls by the barrelful will turn up, some of them half a century old and long past any degree of usefulness.   Among them will often be balls of white made of flour sacks, chicken feed bags, and other lowly materials, awaiting the benison of the dye pot.

Possibly the oldest, and possibly also the most beautiful carpeting which may be called Pennsylvania Dutch is one which is becoming increasingly hard to secure.   This is the linen carpeting, woven in the same way as the other, but in its natural cream or tan coloring. In strong contrast to this neutral tone are brilliant bands near the edges, perhaps six or eight inches wide, created by colored warp threads. Sometimes the effects are quite garish, as when combinations of orange, red, and purple were used, but very frequently more pleasing blends occur. Then, too, time has softened the brilliance of colors that must once have clashed violently, so that the effect is less positive than it sounds on paper. Carpeting of this sort without worn spots is hard to find, so that it is seldom one sees it except in rather short strips. Still, it is not impossible to secure enough of one kind to cover even a good-sized floor.

Walls and Hangings

THE day when walls were merely something to hang pictures on has fortunately passed, although it is safe to say that not one person in ten makes the most of the unique decorative opportunities inherent in walls, doorways, and windows. The architectural form of an old Pennsylvania Dutch house is one which admitted of little variation; and the person who tampers too much in achieving variation within an architectural form may lose considerably more than he gains. The same thing is not necessarily true of an interior treatment, for there were as many possibilities as there were householders, and taste and caprice were responsible for the little touches that gave homes their individuality.

Many persons seeking to re-create an atmosphere of earlier days turn to wall paper, with its skillful reproductions of older patterns, as the proper solution of the difficulty imposed by bare walls. Wall paper has much to recommend it, particularly in town houses or apartments and in frame houses in the country. But the stone house dweller will find to his sorrow that unless he goes to the tremendous expense of building what amounts to new walls inside all his old ones wall paper simply will not stick. The dampness which is almost inevitable on stone walls will sooner or later cause the paper to let go in great, unsightly strips. A single inside wall may often be papered with fair success, but not if the house is to be shut up over the winter or left unheated for any length of time. Calcium chloride placed in satisfactory containers helps to eliminate dampness, but it is by no means a cure-all.

After wall paper, paint is the usual solution, with a choice of the oil and casein varieties. Of these, casein is apt to be the more satisfactory, for it will stick after oil paint has begun to shale off. This applies, of course, to plastered surfaces. Wood will take oil paint with little or no trouble.

When an old house is being restored an effort ought to be made to see whether or not, under the successive layers of red or brown or green there is not an original coat of the old, soft Dutch blue. If the blue coat is there, it is worth making an effort to bring it to light and preserve it, for it is definitely a pleasing and authentic touch. If the old blue is not to be found, an off-white coating is usually the safest choice, for it offers the best foil for the painted furniture and other decorated objects the householder will wish to display. A rough plaster finish generally looks better than a smooth one, particularly if it is to be left unpainted.

To secure as much painted wooden surface as possible for background, built-in cupboards, corner or otherwise, are a great help. Not only may the proportions of a given room often benefit by having an entire end given over to cupboards, but the rest of the furnishings will also show to better advantage against this painted background. Book cases may be built in, whether at the end of a room or around a doorway, and open painted shelves for the housing of special collections may often be combined with them.

Glass shelves in sunny windows have come to be all but commonplace, but are still one of the best means of gaining sparkling color in a room. In the deep windows of the old stone houses they seem especially at home. Plate rails often help rather plain wall expanses, and are ideal for keeping attractive pieces of tôle or copper or china visible but out of the way. "Picture" windows where there is an especially fine view have much to commend them, particularly if the frame of the picture possesses an inherent attractiveness when the view outside is not in evidence.

Admittedly, built-in cupboards or shelves or plate rails are not peculiarly Pennsylvania Dutch; in fact they are in most cases not Pennsylvania Dutch at all, except in the sense that a Pennsylvania Dutchman who felt the need for any of them in his home was enough of a craftsman to build them forthwith. The home owner of today, however, is most vitally concerned with what to put into his house and how to display it to best advantage, and to that end he is justified in taking any reasonable steps to provide a creditable and satisfactory background.

Walls, whether they are old or new, painted or papered, must be utilized in order to display certain Pennsylvania Dutch art forms properly. There are, first of all, the *Handtuchen*, or fancy towels, those elaborate forerunners of the modern guest towels. Almost always of a fine quality of homespun linen, these towels were adorned with handwork embellishments in white as well as in blue, red, and occasionally other colors. In a sense the decorations suggest those of some early samplers, with their rows of conventionalized floral designs, representations of birds, animals and human figures, and the name of the maker, together with the date of execution.

Cross-stitching was the favorite method of carrying out the design, although the whole repertoire of needlework possibilities seems to have been brought in to play. The door towels were originally for show, and were used as covers for the very unromantic, everyday roller towel. In Europe, particularly in Switzerland, there was a painted or stenciled case built purposely to accommodate these towels, but no example of any such creation has as yet been identified in Pennsylvania.

Rather sizable collections of *Handtuchen* have been made in recent years, and they have been written up for the magazines (with a consequent boost in price!) but as yet no means of displaying them has been discovered better than the original one: hanging them on the wall. They may be thumb-tacked to doors or judiciously placed in hall, bedroom, or elsewhere. Their naïve charm is such that they add a warm and intimate note to almost any surface they grace. Considering the price that one pays nowadays for even fair specimens, one hesitates to suggest that they make unusual and distinctive table runners.

Mirrors are an extremely important decorative adjunct in the Pennsylvania Dutch setting, not only because they are relatively inexpensive but because of their beauty and their strong individuality. The type which first comes to mind is perhaps the mahogany veneered, ogee-curved one, so many frames of which seem to have been preserved in attics, woodsheds, and barns long after the mirror itself had been cracked or destroyed entirely. Refinishing an old mirror frame is a relatively simple task, and is often the starting-point of the beginner. The original glass is a definite asset when it is to be found in usable condition, but for dressing tables, especially, a modern replacement is considerably less strain on one's disposition. These mahogany veneered frames have a softwood base underneath, and the mellow pine, when neatly finished, is almost as attractive as the finer cabinet wood. For rooms in which pine furniture predominates, pine mirrors unveneered are a first choice.

Not long ago a rather remarkable mirror embodying a combination of pine and mahogany was offered for sale. A first reaction to the striking combination of amber and brown was that it had originally been completely veneered, but that, in the refinishing, narrow sections of the veneer had been discarded. The extremely narrow surfaces of pine molding at the very edge of the glass, however, made such a procedure seem doubtful. Whatever its genesis, it is certainly a satisfying way of tying together dark and light furniture in a room where complete furnishing with one type is not feasible. Moreover, with the abundant supply of veneered frames available, the combination offers one solution to a problem which has puzzled many a decorator.

Very attractive, too, are mirror frames of walnut. There seems to be a greater range of sizes in these than in mahogany, and, because they have not always been as highly regarded as mahogany, are occasionally to be had at a lower figure. Ogee curves are less common in walnut than are plane surfaces. Eighteen inches by twenty-four is a usual size for a mahogany ogee frame, but greater dimensions are quite common. Very desirable are the large frames which may be used horizontally above a davenport or a fireplace mantel. On the other hand, the range in walnut frames is usually downward from a maximum of about eighteen by twenty-four inches.

Definitely hard to find but worth the trouble, nevertheless, are tin-framed mirrors. Punched tin lanterns are by no means uncommon, and tin pie safes can still be secured, but mirror frames of punched tin are rarities. For one thing they were very early, seemingly antedating the wooden frames. It seems reasonable to suppose that, once walnut was found desirable, the cruder, home-made tin pieces were done away with. One noteworthy specimen is circular in shape, with an over-all diameter of about sixteen inches. It was created of two pieces neatly soldered together, and is cut out in the center to make room for a mirror about nine inches in diameter. The elements of decoration consist first of a series of lunettes bordering the mirror edge, and, beyond these, rayed circles. These patterns are punched merely, not pierced. Attached to the edge of the tin frame are individual punched circular tin discs slightly more than an inch across, forming a complete border for the piece. The lunettes and the centers of the daisy-like circular designs are filled in alternately with vermilion and soft green paint. The present mirror glass is a replacement. A somewhat similar mirror, but of rectangular design, was offered for sale at a shop in Connecticut several years ago. It was of established Pennsylvania provenance, however.

In the luxury class are the popularly-titled "courting" mirrors, those small objects with veneered, polychromed, or painted frames which sailors long ago brought back from China for the ladies of their choice. Those most in demand seem to be the ones with bits of ingenuous hand painting—floral designs or other simple representation—incorporated under glass as a separate unit above the mirror. The painting (generally done on the reverse of the glass itself) was sometimes repeated on narrow panels of glass set into the mirror frame. Now and then one of these mirrors in its original box is to be found, with a price so staggering as to remind the buyer of its extreme scarcity.

More to the taste of the layman is the "painted glass" mirror, the kind with a looking-glass at the bottom and a bit of rural scenery painted either on the surface or the reverse of a glass panel above. They usually have turned frames with an architectural molding across the top. They are to be found in various conditions of desirability, albeit with many of the choicest specimens already in museums. Factors to consider are the fineness of detail of the painted panel at the top; the simplicity and good proportions of the frame; and the condition of the mirror itself. Since almost any piece of Pennsylvania Dutch furniture is salable if it has even a small trace of the original painting intact, it would be foolish to quibble too much over the condition of the painted panel. At the same time, a mirror is so steadily in one's line of vision that its condition is bound to be a matter of awareness. Under the circumstances, it would appear that only a really good specimen is worth a sizeable investment. In any case, it is not a bad idea to have a modern, full-length looking-glass in the house, on the inside of a convenient closet door, for instance.

Another type of wall ornamentation which is practically mandatory for the Pennsylvania house is the colored pen painting, or fractur work. This art form, seemingly indigenous to Pennsylvania, is a remote survival of the ancient European art of manuscript illumination. It ranges from the crude work of the untrained layman to the painstaking, even elaborate efforts of those who spent long hours in attempting to achieve perfection. Perhaps the finest fractur work ever done on this side the Atlantic was in the Sister House of the monastery at Ephrata, Pennsylvania, where the walls bore specimens of all-but-perfect illuminated lettering.

For the householder there are a number of forms available, of considerable range in quality but all of guileless charm. First there are the hand-made birth and baptismal certificates, with the proper data filled in in painfully neat German script. Not infrequently this part of the certificate was contained within the outline of a large heart, beyond the borders of which were flowers or birds, and angelic forms hovering benevolently near. The pen and ink outlines of the figures were done first and then filled in with colors, many of which have retained their original intensity to a remarkable degree. The size of these documents was generally about twelve by fifteen inches, large enough, when framed with a generous-sized mat, for a very satisfactory wall decoration.

Ideally, of course, one should be able to display a birth certificate which has come down through successive generations of his family. So delightful, however, are the primitive artistic representations on all such certificates that one never passes up a specimen, no matter how badly worn it may be. Market values on these *Geburts- und Taufscheine* continue to rise, and even small fragments have their prices. The oldest forms are, as might be expected, in pretty bad condition unless they have been kept flat. Those dating earlier than 1800 are frequently almost impossible to handle. Fly leaves of printed or handmade song books and account books, as well as documents other than birth and baptismal certificates, were frequently illuminated.

A later form of *Taufschein* appeared about the middle of the nineteenth century. With its decorative outlines stamped by the printing press, it was at once a boon to the unskilled penman and an admission that the art of illumination had all but died out in German Pennsylvania. It required no more skill than that possessed by a small child to fill in the outlines of birds, cherries, leaves, and angels with any color that fancy dictated. Yet even here there was a peculiar individual touch in the addition of a freehand plaid design in an angel's robe, or a spot of color in the cheeks, that makes one willing to part with the few dollars required to become the owner of one of these.

When it is possible, it is a good idea to acquire the original frame in which the certificate was displayed. Many of the very early ones were unframed, and the very late forms were mounted in Victorian trappings at their worst, but even a reasonably good old cherry, walnut, or gilt frame is better than a modern reproduction which fools no one.

This matter of the original frames becomes increasingly important in relation to the other and smaller pieces of fractur work which come up for sale at the shops and shows. Birds, single flowers, square houses with smoke pouring out of the chimneys, human figures all out of perspective—these are the subjects treated. In their little cherry or madder-painted frames, with a brass ring at the top, they lend a touch of rightness to a wall otherwise lacking in distinction. Some of these "pictures" are only a few inches wide and high, and rarely do they approach, say, a ten by twelve inch size. They may be grouped effectively along the wall of a stairway, or for that matter wherever one has a particularly difficult or irregular wall expanse to deal with.

Since large and important pieces of fractur, many of which were reproduced in color in H. S. Borneman's excellent publication a few years ago, are almost inaccessible to the amateur nowadays, he will do well to borrow a trick from the antiques dealer, who immediately riffles the pages of the old Bibles he comes upon. It was between the covers of the great family Bible that the hand-done awards of merit, Sunday School cards, and other tokens of the teacher's approbation were kept when the children brought them home. Not infrequently such cards can be grouped satisfactorily and framed, with a resultant creation that could not be duplicated commercially.

Yet another individual wall decoration is the old-time valentine, which in German Pennsylvania was a paper cut-out, rivaling in intricacy the tracings on lacy Sandwich glass. The effect was presumably achieved with a knife blade of razor-sharpness. Early forms were usually of white paper, on which an inscription of properly romantic nature was elaborately inscribed. Beautifully detailed doves, hearts, and flowers were usually the elements of design. In later years the paper cut-outs became cruder, finally giving way to the ornate creations of the Victorian period. Since the paper valentines are exceedingly fragile, it is a good idea to mount them on a bit of dark fabric and frame them. Only when they are behind glass can one be sure that the delicate tracery of fern or bird's wing will not be destroyed by a well-meaning but damaging caress.

Speaking of the Victorian valentine, one might mention a related form which can be used to good advantage as a wall decoration: the richly colorful lithographed friendship card of the eighties and nineties, and even later. These little cards, with their fringed borders, doves, baskets of flowers, heart-and-hand combinations, and choice "sentiments," may be arranged in groups behind glass, and there provide a spot of color far removed from the banal commercial print.

Still other manifestations of the Pennsylvania Dutch creative spirit are to be found. Samplers were almost as common in Pennsylvania as in New England, and make good wall pieces. The later Victorian commercial samplers which bore such phrases as "God Bless Our Home" and "What Is Home Without a Mother?" are now and then surprisingly attractive. Until lately there was little demand for them, and they can often be obtained very reasonably. Their walnut frames, with sprays of leaves cut out of wood and glued across the corners, were as indispensable to the country parlor as a fancy lambrequin or a hair wreath.

Steadily growing in popularity is the Pennsylvanian painting-on-glass. This was a somewhat unconventional art form, in which the color was applied directly to the reverse surface of the glass. The painters were almost certainly non-professional, although now and then really meritorious work is found, work which evidences a certain skill and command of technique. Favorite subjects were important historical figures, such as Washington, Jefferson, Lafayette, and Andrew Jackson. Sometimes a name was supplied, but oftener not, as presumably the person portrayed was so well known as to need no identification. With the recent revival of interest in primitive portraiture, these paintings have doubled and trebled in price. Historical personages are most sought for, with an unaccountable customer-predilection for Napoleon and Lafayette. Among feminine portraits those whose costumes are enriched with lace are especially popular, the successful reproduction on glass of an intricate lace pattern being something of a test of skill. The art of painting on glass is said to have originated in China.

"Tinsel" pictures, too, are found in Pennsylvania as in New York or New England or Virginia. It is a question as to where they actually did originate, but they are decidedly at home in the stone house. These "pictures" were clusters of flowers behind glass. Spots on the reverse of the glass, the size of the flowers to be represented, were lightly painted red or yellow or blue. Back of each spot a piece of crinkly gold or silver tinsel was secured, so that the effect at a little distance was that of radiantly luminous flower forms. The customary background or mat for the grouping was black, the whole creation being framed in gilt.

The householder will also probably wish to investigate the matter of the "pioneer" art work done in the early days when America was becoming art-conscious. Works in oils and in other media are available. The beginner might well consult Drepperd's *American Pioneer Arts and Artists* for ideas.

Leaving the subject of framed wall ornaments, one thinks immediately of the old-time tôle trays, which produce an effect of richness when hung in the proper light. These trays will be discussed in a later chapter.

For very large wall spaces there are the woven coverlets which were mentioned earlier. They are at their best when mounted securely on a rod and hung where they can be seen in their entirety. Even the tyro will realize, of course, that it is only in exceptional instances that so large a piece can be used satisfactorily: in a hall or on a landing of unusual size or proportions; on a completely unbroken wall expanse, perhaps behind a davenport or Dutch bench; or most logically dropped from a picture molding at the head of a low bed.

Still another satisfactory wall treatment can be achieved through the use of hooked rugs, from the exquisitely done little mats to be found on the Gaspé Peninsula in Canada to the large ones of the antique shops and, latterly, the roadside stands of rural Pennsylvania. There is a sense of fitness about these hooked designs that makes them seem at home on walls of rooms using simple furniture and colorful accessories. In general, it is wise to use only new ones on walls, since the faded or muted tones of the older ones are apt to appear dingy against lighter backgrounds.

A word might be said about draperies for the deep windows which are indubitably one of the greatest charms of the stone house. One may re-create various other features of the Pennsylvania Dutchman's domicile with reasonable success, but windows with two-feet-deep seats have thus far defied imitation. Generally the sides and top of the window orifice have been neatly paneled, and no draperies should be used which would render any of their beauty invisible. Among genuinely old fabrics which have been used successfully for this purpose are various coarsely-woven linens, cottons, gingham and other materials. Narrow lengths of hand-woven coverlets which were damaged in spots have been salvaged for this purpose, as have sections taken from old patchwork quilts or quilted spreads. In some instances plain muslin or linen has been bordered with old fabrics with pleasing effect. Department stores now offer "Provincial" motifs which fit in well with most simple settings. The careful shopper may find roses, hearts and tulips in a wide variety of fabrics and weaves.

Lamps

WORTH considerably more attention than might at first be supposed, are the lamps to be used in the Pennsylvania Dutch house. In fact, good lamps can go far toward harmonizing conflicting elements which have to be tolerated for one reason or another; and fortunate indeed is the person who has never had to get along with a chair or table which in his secret heart he yearns to destroy. After dark the lamp calls attention both to itself and to the table on which it rests; therefore it should be placed not only where it will be useful but where it will serve a dramatic purpose. By day it will have to stand on its own merits as a decorative adjunct to the room.

The problem of electric lighting fixtures is one to which unfortunately there is as yet no really satisfactory solution. Wall or ceiling fixtures were unheard of in the days of the tulip and the lily, and the best that can be done will necessarily be an anachronism. The same thing holds true, of course, for Colonial fixtures, with the important difference that modern creations in the Colonial feeling are being manufactured while as yet there has been little call for Pennsylvania Dutch adaptations.

The best solution is to eliminate all wall or ceiling fixtures which are not absolutely necessary, and to use the simplest New England Colonial where elimination is impossible. Fixtures in brass, in copper, and in tôle can be obtained, many of them in good, and what is chiefly significant here, in unobtrusive designs. Anyone who can use a built-in system of indirect lighting will be free from fixture-worry, although he may have spent enough to buy a dozen really superlative lamps.

It is assumed that only a museum would be interested in the old fat lamps, Betty-lamps, and the like as a means of illumination, and only those which have decorative qualities are suggested here. Among very early forms there is the so-called "Paul Revere" tin lantern, a pierced tin cylinder with conical top and hinged door, made to accommodate a candle. The tin was pierced in a geometrical design, the perforations being usually of dots and dashes, with the rough edges outside. Most antique shops are able to produce one or two of them, although sometimes they are too badly rusted to be really usable. In good condition they fit in well with the best of Pennsylvania Dutch furniture, and are especially effective in rooms which also contain a pierced tin pie safe or tin mirror.   If they are to serve only as objects of art it might be better not to electrify them.   Wired, they are especially effective in hallways, or at either side of an entrance.   They should not, of course, be fully exposed to the weather.   Numerous patterns have been found, the rayed circle design perhaps being most satisfying.   No peculiar merit attaches to any design, the condition of the tin being of first importance.   They are very early, but such humble articles were not generally considered worth dating.

Another early form which can be wired and used with primitive furniture is the candle mold.   This curious reversal of affairs—using the mold instead of the candle—might startle our forbears if they could know about it, and may even seem to us like a straining after the bizarre or the quaint.   If such is the case, a casual inspection of the offerings of the stores, with their careless approximations of genuine motifs, is usually all that is required to send the householder scurrying to the nearest electrician with his candle mold.

Candlesticks, too, make good lamps, particularly for the dressing table or any place where a small size is desired.   Brass was used in Pennsylvania as frequently as it was elsewhere in the Colonies, and lends itself well to electrification.   More typically Pennsylvanian are candlesticks of mercury glass, particularly those with flowers painted on one side.   There are also candlesticks in brown like the Rockingham ware found in New England, some of them very fine, and others prosaic enough to stand everyday use, while giving a touch of difference to a room.   Candle holders with sconce backs of plain tin or mirrored tin in small segments are useful for console tables, sideboards, or dressing tables, whether electrified or used simply as candlesticks.   With the recent manufacture of devices which may be set into the top of narrow-mouthed jugs, bottles, and candlesticks, it is no longer necessary to damage an antique of value when it is wired.

Dating from early times, too, is the tall floor candlestand, with holders for one or two candles.   This tall stand, of which there are good original specimens in museums, has the virtue of being easily copied by any good ironworker.   It seems to be the only real lighting device of floor-lamp height which has come out of early Colonial times, and as such is worth investigating.   A representative specimen has two candle sockets at the ends of a movable transverse arm.   The stand measures about five feet from the floor to the top of the removable pointed finial.   The rat tails of the sockets and the three gracefully curved legs which support the central shaft contribute to the artistry of the piece, which could be electrified with no sacrifice of beauty.

Lest it seem that the Pennsylvania Dutch had no actual lamps, but only objects which might be made into lamps, one might list a dozen varieties, ranging from the slender, graceful vessels which burned whale oil to the gorgeously decorated Victorian affairs which had reservoirs for upwards of a gallon of kerosene. Just which ones, if any, were distinctive of the Dutchland alone it would be hard to say, but on the evidence of those to be found in old houses, several can be listed with safety.

First, there are those of the familiar pattern glass group, with Lincoln Drape seemingly the most popular design, especially in dark blue. As a matter of fact, there seems to be twice as much Lincoln Drape as any other pattern. These lamps are sometimes low and squatty, with a loop handle at the base, sometimes tall and graceful. They were originally equipped with burner, wick, and glass chimney, but are now easily altered for electricity. Now and then, when an especially beautiful base is found, instead of using the conventional shade, a Czechoslovakian or other glass chimney may be substituted, similar to the chimneys originally intended for such lamps. The Lincoln Drape, of course, is but one of the many pressed glass patterns available. Only individual taste can guide the collector who may be trying to choose among the hobnail variants (now extensively reproduced) or daisy and button, bull's eye, argus, harp, or bellflower. The slender proportions of the earlier whale oil lamps make them particularly appropriate for small desks or dressing tables.

Lamps of old Bohemian glass are effective, especially in rooms where a red and white décor makes it possible to display other Bohemian glass objects—vases, bowls, or liquor bottles. These lamps are often mounted on heavy iron bases. Pairs of them command high prices, but good single specimens are frequently available at a reasonable figure.

The familiar "student" lamp, with its one or two glass shades and its burnished nickel oil reservoir, offers a striking bit of color, whether for an accent or as an object around which to plan a color scheme. Like other glass lamps, it can hardly be called characteristically Pennsylvania Dutch. Common colors are red, yellow, and green.

The ornate Victorian parlor table lamp, or its hanging counterpart, may once more serve a useful purpose if it is well proportioned and its colors are harmonious. It does not often fit mellowly into its surroundings, however, but has a tendency to dominate, thus drawing attention away from more meritorious pieces. In a severely furnished room characterized by a lack of strong design or color it often shows to good advantage.

More worthy of the limelight is the glamorous overlay lamp, with its pink or blue or green cut through to a crystal-clear base. Such a lamp calls for a more sophisticated setting than that of the usual stone house interior, as does its exquisite cousin, the cameo glass lamp. Overlay is most effective with a plain shade which leaves the beauty of the lamp unrivaled.

For night lights or for children's rooms the tiny milk-glass lamps of days gone by are a good choice. The soft blue tones are probably most sought after, and are found more easily than in the taller objects, which, as a matter of fact, are becoming extremely scarce. The Victorian fairy lamps, with their great range of pastel tones, are also excellent for night lights.

On the more prosaic side, but none the less popular, are the various pottery forms which lend a note of rugged honesty and simplicity to any room which contains them. Earthenware in red, brown, or black; in gray or cream color with blue decorations of birds or flowers; in clear glaze, salt glaze, or no glaze at all; in sizes large and small; in pitchers or jars and especially in jugs; earthenware is the first choice of those who want stable lamps of good size, proportions, and coloring. Unlike glass they may be drilled at the base if reasonable care is taken, though no real collector's piece should be thus despoiled merely to get a lamp cord out of the way. Incidentally, a collection of attractive jugs or pitchers which might otherwise have to go begging for lack of satisfactory display space may be used to their ultimate advantage under a permanent mazda spotlight.

Pieces of painted tôleware, too, may be put to good account when wired. Tall coffee pots, tea caddies and canisters may be used in this way, though the collector must realize that under a bright light the colors in the tôle will tend to fade out, at the same time that every minor imperfection will be emphasized. A coffee pot masquerading as a lamp is admittedly on the bizarre side, and the chances are that a better use could be found for it.

For special uses and in special places still other Pennsylvania Dutch accoutrements may serve to shed light on the activities within the house. In a large room the glass carboy which once held wine or vinegar takes on new importance when wired for electricity. The lowly wooden sugar bucket and the heavy tin maple sap bucket have been used as bases for floor lamps. Slender stone Holland gin bottles as well as tall glass bottles of all kinds are invested with new life when given a light bulb and an attractive shade, and are the more satisfactory because they can often be secured in pairs. In fact, the reader would discover, if he could visit all the interiors furnished by collectors, that practically every vessel that will stand upright has been used for a lamp.

Less satisfactory will be the search for shades. There must, of course, be a correlation between the shape and size of the base, and the shade itself. Once the proper shape is found, there remains the matter of color and design, with most of the odds against the Pennsylvania Dutch enthusiast. Plain parchment will serve for some bases, and floral designs for others. The greatest degree of satisfaction, though, will probably come from those created at home out of the proper materials.

A good starting point is an old-time scrap book, the kind filled with highly-colored greeting cards, flowers, animals, cherubs' heads, and the like. Lacking such an heirloom book of his own, the collector can usually pick up one or more at an antique shop or at one of the ubiquitous antique shows. The "pictures" are not hard to remove and, when pasted on plain paper or parchment shades and shellacked, are extremely effective. Costume groups of three quarters of a century ago, groupings of old Christmas or New Year's cards, "friendship" tokens and dozens of other combinations are possible, and for sheer charm and distinction have no equal. Serviceable in like way are old lacy valentines; pen and ink or water color drawings not worthy of a place with fractur; flower prints; scraps of old fabrics or wall paper; pages from old newspapers or books; in fact any pictorial or printed matter possessing antiquarian interest or charm in its own right.

For people gifted with the brush there are dozens of designs to be copied on lamp shades: tulips, pomegranates and flower pots from bride's boxes and dower chests; peacocks and schoolhouses from spatterware; alphabet letters and other devices from samplers; fruit and flower clusters from painted and stenciled furniture; hearts and angels from birth certificates; and innumerable attractive possibilities from woven coverlets, tôleware, Gaudy Dutch plates, enameled Stiegel glass, clock fronts, springerle molds, pattern glass and other sources. It will appear, even to the beginner, that the possibilities are almost endless. Lacking both scrapbooks and the talent for copying, the home decorator may still do well by cutting out and applying figures from the yard goods of Pennsylvania Dutch design now available in stores, or even from floral chintz or cretonne. In any case, decorative matter of this kind should be applied with a strong casein glue, the whole shade then being given a coat of shellac, preferably white. A binding agent less tenacious than the casein glue is apt to loosen under the heat of the light bulb.

Clocks

If the reader whose daily routine or any portion of it is geared to an exact schedule of hours and minutes, let it be said at once that his Pennsylvania Dutch house should contain at least one electric clock—and preferably two, one in the bathroom and one in the kitchen. It might as well be admitted at the outset that he whose hours are measured solely by the chimes of an old clock will come to regret that fact sooner or later. Those old clocks not infrequently represented a substantial original investment and were, therefore, customarily retained as long as they gave satisfactory service. It stands to reason that many of them, no matter how beautiful, are by now thoroughly worn out and, in spite of the glib assurances of dealers, cannot be perfectly rejuvenated.

If, knowing that he may expect to spend the rest of his life administering to the needs of clocks which must be wound regularly (and not too near the hour lest they strike prematurely); which are prone to gain or lose for no apparent reason; which in some cases call for the services of an erratic and highly-paid specialist at disconcertingly frequent intervals—if the householder wishes to do the proper thing by his house and give it an old timepiece for every room, he has an abundance of beautiful forms from which to choose. Let him consider well the end, however; the inevitable question on the lips of every visitor will be: "What a remarkable clock! *Does it run?*" It calls for a Spartan disposition to face that question, and the man who invariably answers it in the affirmative is a logical candidate for the Ananias Club.

Most important of them all is the tall case or "grandfather" clock, about which a great deal has been said and written. It is increasingly difficult to buy one nowadays, either from the owners to whose hearts they are dear, or at the auction sales where the bidding is fierce and determined. Yet fine specimens are to be had now and then, when, for the first time, they are removed from the home in which their all-but-forgotten first owner so proudly placed them. What the purchaser may expect to receive will depend largely on what he is willing to pay. As they are of individual craftsmanship, hardly two are identical, even when executed by the same maker. Some are well-proportioned, others excessively tall, and still others distressingly broad and massive. Some of the faces are bright and open, others dingy and secretive. Exquisite ornamentation and decorative detail lend charm in some, while others are characterized by stark simplicity or obvious crudity. Choice specimens run to fancy figures, but honest and meritorious examples are to be had at what our contemporary civilization has come to call "budget" prices.

For the stone house a good choice would be a fruit-wood case with a dial painted in corner designs of flower clusters and surmounted by a colorful bird. Ideally the flowers should be tulips and the bird a peacock, but such a combination does not often occur. Ornamentation of this kind was sometimes done in the rural counties of Pennsylvania, and its charm is on a par with that of painted and stenciled furniture. One known dial of this kind is found in a walnut case, and the muted rose and green of the flower clusters with the resplendent bird above harmonize mellowly with the rich glow of the dark wood. Undated, it is of about the years 1790 to 1800. The case itself has neatly reeded posts, a concave circular panel at the base, and a bonnet surmounted by a single brass finial. Over all, it stands eighty-eight inches high.

The height of one's ceilings, needless to say, will often prove the deciding factor in a contemplated purchase, and wise is he who is prepared, when far away from home, to state definitely that his ceiling is eighty-four or ninety or a hundred inches from the floor. If he trusts to luck he may be reduced to the expedient adopted by a collector who was compelled to stand her clock in the middle of the room, with its bonnet protruding through an open trapdoor above! Scarcely less distressing is the sight of a fine old clock seemingly crammed into a corner, its topmost finial wholly or partly amputated, with the result that it looks as though it had pierced the ceiling. So many old clocks are so tall that it might be said that their makers regarded the sky as the limit.

The choice of wood in the grandfather's clock will largely be determined by the nature of the furniture in the room. An elaborate mahogany case would make simple pine or maple furniture suffer by contrast, although it would go well with walnut, mahogany, or fine painted pieces. Museums and historical rooms have so often featured choice specimens in the dark woods that the beginner has not always realized that he has a reasonable chance of discovering a tall case clock in pine, butternut, poplar, apple, or pear wood. Less imposing than the others, these specimens often possess a charm and grace of line that has nothing to do with their novelty.

It has been argued that complicated mechanisms indicating the changes of the season, phases of the moon, and the like, are out of keeping with the fundamental simplicity of the furnishings of the Pennsylvania Dutch home. There may be an element of truth in the idea, but it may also be borne in mind that the tall case clock was frequently the finest and most expensive piece of furniture in the entire house. If the proportions are pleasing, the wood satisfactory, and the general appearance such that it will lend distinction to the room without making the rest of its furniture seem rude, there is no good reason why even the most elaborate combinations of mechanical ingenuity should not be given an honored place. The buyer should familiarize himself with the peculiar capacities of his clock at the outset, however, so that he may know just what to expect. Incidentally, the tyro is sometimes startled at the discovery that the most sedate and dignified clock possesses a loud, high-pitched chime rather than the mellifluous tone he had expected to hear. Too, he may be disconcerted to learn that many early specimens are thirty-hour, not eight-day clocks.

As in the case of other furniture, those clocks which are signed and dated are considered most desirable, but many an unauthenticated Pennsylvania painted dial has found a home before its fully documented companion. It is largely a matter of the inherent beauty of the piece. Names of clockmakers in the Dutchland include Emanuel Meyli, Charles Cooper, and Jacob Guthert of Lebanon; Joseph Fix, Daniel Oyster, Benjamin Whitman, and Johan Hahn of Reading; John Esterle of New Holland; and E. Zimmerman, George Breneisen, and Martin Shreiner among still others. According to tradition, Shreiner produced no fewer than two hundred and seventy-four clocks, numbered consecutively from the first one in 1783. It is said that his output was twelve a year.

Tall case clocks, more commonly out of, than in Pennsylvania, were occasionally found in small sizes, which are usually referred to as "grandmother" clocks. These are customarily about four feet high and closely resemble the taller forms.

Fully as distinctive as either the grandfather or the grandmother type is its immediate predecessor, the wag-on-the-wall, which is said to have originated in Holland toward the end of the seventeenth century. In this specimen the dial, pendulum, and, in fact, the entire mechanism are without a wooden case. It is the dial which, gaudily decorated with clusters or festoons of roses, gives it a place in the stone farmhouse. The rosaceous ornamentation marks it as kin with other painted and decorated pieces. If it is true, as some writers maintain, that the white-painted dial was not known before 1790, then those specimens of the wag-on-the-wall now to be obtained are of later creation than many of the tall case clocks, since most of the floral designs are imposed on a white background. By virtue of their size and imposing appearance, all these clocks demand important or strategic positions in the house, frequently in hallways or on broad landings.

Among the not unimposing array of other timepieces which have survived the years, several are eminently suited to the needs of the Pennsylvania Dutch

WALNUT CLOCK WITH PAINTED DIAL

PIERCED TIN PIE CUPBOARD

interior. The well-known shelf clocks of the 1830's, 1840's and later years, ranging in height from perhaps fifteen inches to almost three feet, are to be had by the collector of even very modest means. Their works of brass were turned out in what might be called mass production, with the result that families which had never been able to afford a tall case clock might easily possess a half dozen of the new variety if they wished. The story of the Connecticut clockmakers and the names of Curtis, Willard, Manross, Ingraham, Seth Thomas, and Eli Terry are too well known to call for amplification here. It is perhaps sufficient to say that the timepieces themselves, with their Roman-figured dials, neatly veneered cases, and painted glass panels will do credit to any fireplace mantel, Welsh dresser, or chest of drawers.

Mahogany and rosewood veneer over pine or some other softwood are oftenest to be found, though occasionally superb bird's-eye maple veneer in combination with one of the other two is seen. When properly refinished, no more beautiful, mellow glow can be produced on any veneered surface than on these excellent bits of cabinetwork. For the person working with a definite color scheme in mind, the fact that the painted glass panel constituting the lower part of the door is usually in a solid background color is of importance. Indeed, the whole color scheme of the room may be suggested by the door panel. For example, one little clock boasts a golden squirrel sharply outlined against a muted red background. It is not hard to visualize this clock in a bedroom with a yellow painted and stenciled dresser, a wooden chair or two with gilt stenciling, and a red and white old-fashioned patchwork quilt used as a counterpane. In a study furnished in pine, a tallish clock in bird's-eye maple veneer provides a focal point with its painted panel of soft golden greens and blues in a Chinese scene. Most striking of all, perhaps, is a red-brown mahogany clock with a luminous blue panel, in a cherry bedroom in which a lamp, a vase, and various dresser pieces are in soft blue milk glass of matching tone. The design against the background is a pair of lyres exquisitely outlined in white. The designs employed cover a wide range, but dogs, squirrels, birds, and flowers are frequently met with. The "Chinese View" mentioned above is a reflection of a period in which the Chinese element was extremely popular in decoration. Likewise to be found are representations of historic events. These are worth serious consideration, although they are not usually colorful. The condition of the painting itself will challenge the buyer, who will do well to open the door and make a careful inspection of the paint. Almost all authentic examples are likely to show signs of wear, with more bits of color chipped away than will appear from the outside. Since there is no particular shortage of this type of clock, it may be assumed that one may turn down with a minimum of regret either a retouched specimen or one with the design seriously marred.

Among shelf clocks the so-called Gothic style, with its graceful upward conic projections at the corners and its pointed top is outstanding. This design is usually attributed to Ingraham of Connecticut. Occasional fantastic variations of the Gothic pattern turn up, indicating that some rural clockmaker had been trying his hand at a variation of a model grown monotonous to him. The taste of the buyer will have to guide him here, and will undoubtedly lead him to reject too-obvious cases of trying to gild the lily.

Still other clocks, beautiful or meritorious in themselves, will demand attention. French clocks, marble clocks, ormolu clocks, banjo clocks and, in fact, an almost infinite variety of timepieces will sound their siren call, and while the decorator may hesitate momentarily, if he will but consider the simple line and peasant origin of much of his furniture, the homeliness of his art objects, he will eschew what could easily be a disturbing element and stick to the weights hung upon strings, the little angular keys, and the engaging simplicity of the American shelf clock.

Boxes and Baskets

SOMEONE, probably the wife of an inveterate collector, once said that no house ever has enough storage space, and few are the hardy and orderly souls who would challenge the statement. In the days when stone houses were new, rooms were simply closetless, and extra clothing was either relegated to the clothes press or, more often, to the spare bedroom. Whatever else that was not intended for immediate use was safely stowed away in a variety of chests and boxes that are a constant source of delight to the later generation which finds the stone house still closetless. The *kas*, the tall chest of drawers, and the dower chest have been mentioned in earlier pages. There remains a fascinating array of smaller receptacles, some largely utilitarian, others veritable works of art, but all of them interesting and useful.

If one had but a single choice among the smaller pieces, he would undoubtedly select the painted bride's box, the origin of which is probably European. Competent authorities aver that most, if not all, of these gaily bedizened receptacles came from Europe, Switzerland in particular. Be that as it may, they are indissolubly linked with early days and ways in Pennsylvania, and are hardly to be met with outside Penn's counties. Bride's boxes are in the shape of an elongated oval, ranging in depth from about ten inches to eighteen, and in length from twelve to twenty-four. They are of a light wood stretched about an oval base, to which they are attached by small nails or pegs. The single piece of which the frame itself is made is secured at one side by an ingeniously contrived wooden withe or rawhide thong. The lid of the box is similarly constructed, and fits down over the framework to a depth of an inch or more.

Tradition has it that the box was the gift of the prospective bridegroom to his bride, and in it the lady kept the choicer or more fragile items of her trousseau. The decorations of the boxes would often seem to bear out such an assumption, for male and female figures hand in hand usually dominate the upper surface of the lid. According to the skill of the artist, they sometimes appear coyly romantic, but just as often stiff and uncompromisingly rigid of countenance. One choice specimen, bearing the "German" inscription *"Ich liebe dich mit luff"* ("I love you with love") depicts a bridal pair of such determined, even ferocious mien that it is easy to see why the artist

71

felt impelled to add the explanatory caption. The costumes are those of the late eighteenth century. The rest of the box is completely covered with pomegranates, tulips, and conventional designs in red, blue, green, yellow, and brown. A few of the finer bride's boxes are dated, most of them in the late 1700's. Not all of them have the bride and groom motif. Many of them are done entirely in flowers, fruit, and conventionalized design, and are fully as attractive as the others, even though less highly prized by connoisseurs.

Since such boxes are rather too large to use purely as *objets d'art*, but at the same time too precious to be subjected to hard usage unless they are in the very best of condition, they now often serve as receptacles for such varied articles as lingerie, handkerchiefs, gloves, or papers. A fine specimen would do credit to a buffet in a pine or maple dining room.

In descending scale of size, there is a long line of boxes similar in design and construction but without polychrome ornamentation which will meet the need or whim of the buyer. Some are so small that they will house no more than a few papers of matches; others will accommodate buttons, pencils, postage stamps, paper clips, writing paper, or any number of prosaic household articles. These small boxes, usually in the rough, have all but been overlooked by most collectors, with the result that they may be secured very reasonably. Often they are covered with coats of wallpaper. Again they are heavily encrusted with paint. In the refinishing, one can never be sure just what will emerge from the most ordinary looking specimen. Sometimes it is a mere fragile shell, but again it may be a little maple box so solid that it will bear the weight of a man. Nesting sets of dry measures, bound in metal, sometimes lend themselves to domestic uses, although they do not have the handmade charm of the small ones, now generally called bureau boxes.

Boxes or "safes" for homemade candles are often decorated, if one may apply the term "often" to an article so seldom found. Of simple rectangular construction, a representative specimen is about ten inches wide, nine deep, and twelve long. Its top is a panel sliding smoothly in grooves cut into the sides. Its decorations consist of tulips in white and the familiar dark gray-blue of Pennsylvania, the whole on a dull orange background. In contradistinction to many old housewares in poor condition, painted boxes of this sort, as well as the bride's boxes, are worth acquiring in almost any state of preservation. They are simple enough to lend themselves readily to restoration, and it would be folly to turn down even a fairly dilapidated specimen just because it needed considerable attention. This is one of the rare cases in the antique world where half a loaf is definitely better than no bread.

To be found only in the heart of the Dutchland is the tiny "house" box, so called because its proportions suggest those of a severe frame dwelling. For that matter it might just as well be called a "trunk" box, for its gently curved lid, fastening with a midget latch, suggests the old fashioned trunk as much as it does a house. Boxes of this sort are painted a solid color—yellow or russet or green, over which tulips or other flowers are sometimes scattered. Bits of landscape are shown on some, and in occasional instances decalcomania garlands have been used. As much because of their scarcity as their beauty, these little boxes, just large enough to hold two packs of cigarettes or two decks of cards, command top prices.

Unique among Pennsylvania Dutch polychromed boxes is a specimen which bears on its lid an exact replica of the six-petaled red and blue open tulip design of spatterware. The box, which rests on a projecting base and has a slightly projecting hinged cover, carries the inscription "Emma Billig, 1810." The background color is a dark brown, and an over-all spiral design has been lightly applied with a small spatter sponge. The four corners of the lid have been marked off in quadrants, and the space filled in with red and white paint. Aside from its mere attractiveness, this box is important in that it offers a pure spatterware design at a date somewhat earlier than the time usually thought of in connection with spatter.

Some antiques dealers seem to have unusual luck in securing for their trade a fairly steady supply of ornamental boxes, round, oval, square, and oblong in shape. That they are of American origin in all cases is open to some doubt, although they are part and parcel of the peasant urge toward ornamentation that has given us most of our appealing painted wares. Not dissimilar objects in Germany, in Switzerland, in Sweden, and perhaps elsewhere suggest that, like the bride's boxes, many of them may have come from the old countries in the past. Of the local provenance of the candle safe alone may one feel fairly sure; for the rest it is safest not to jump to conclusions before positive proof comes to light. In the meantime it is comforting to reflect that even recent imported peasant wares, noticeably those from Sweden, often command higher prices in the department stores than do the genuinely old ones in the antique shops.

Another "box" which has made its appearance in many a country home recently is the ancient dough tray, in which the housewife kneaded the family supply of bread and then put it in a warm place to rise. The dough tray was often mounted on trestle or stretcher legs for convenience in handling, but some specimens were evidently intended to be placed on the kitchen table when in use. In their present department store reincarnation they appear as tables with the top removable, thus revealing capacious depths for the storing of magazines or books. The authentic ones are ordinarily of plain pine, without paint or decoration, and when refinished possess a distinction that their slick, mass production counterparts fall short of achieving. A very few originals, however, with paneled designs not unlike those to be found on dower chests, have been discovered. A typical dough box is of inch-thick pine boards, about ten inches wide at the bottom, sloping outward to about fourteen at the top. It is ten inches deep and three feet long, and has a sliding cover with a simple wooden handle. Not too versatile a piece, it belongs with the simplest furniture of the household. One young woman uses hers to store lengths of dress goods, thread, and patterns, against the day when she feels the urge to do some sewing.

Wallpaper covered cardboard boxes of considerable antiquity, for all their fragile nature, are often found in surprisingly good condition. Many of these were bonnet boxes, and accommodated headgear from the simple coverings of the Plain People to the elaborate creations of the worldly. As might be expected, there is a marked range in size. It would call for some intrepidity on the part of a collector to acquire more than one or two of these ancient hat boxes, for they are bulky, fragile, and not too useful. The greatest part of their charm lies, of course, in the wall paper which embraces everything from imported French paper of the 1700's or early 1800's to the offerings of the mail order era. Occasionally an important historical scene is shown, as in the case of a dealer who discovered that he had, on a paper hat box, the earliest known representation of City Hall in New York. Now and then in the shop of a rural dealer one will find row upon row of these boxes in a loft, patiently awaiting their inevitable destruction. Looking at their torn covers and dingy bulges one cannot help but feel that, with few exceptions, they should have been mercifully destroyed years ago. The best of them have long since gravitated to the museums or to private collections. To be sure, there is always the chance that something really worth while may turn up, notably at auctions of households where things have always been well cared for.

Fully as appealing as old boxes, although less versatile in use, are the baskets of the Dutchland. The white oak egg baskets, shaped like a half globe or melon, are outstanding for their sturdy construction, their broad, tightly-woven splints defying the ravages of time to a remarkable degree. They range in size from midgets three inches in diameter to giants of more than two feet. Needless to say, their owners used them for many purposes besides carrying eggs. Studying their hemispherical construction one is forced to conclude that the farmers' wives who originally owned them must always have kept them suspended by their stout handles, for they tilt disastrously at the slightest touch when placed on a flat surface. Anyone who succumbs to their charm nowadays, thinking of the desk that cries for a wastebasket, will find one solution in standing the basket over a low earthenware pot.

Not all these baskets have handles. Some are low and broad, their splints so tightly woven that they would hold wheat or rye without spilling a grain. A roadside basketmaker who sold his wares in Northampton

County up to just a few years ago proportioned his so that they would contain an even half bushel. Those which ran slightly larger or smaller he would sell at a reduced rate, thus innocently laying the foundation for a good deal of neighborhood trouble. Eventually he discontinued his occupation because, as he impatiently explained, so many city people who could have no possible use for them wanted his baskets that he could not supply local needs, and he felt that he was wasting his time! Only a few decades ago the making of these baskets for sale was a common winter evening occupation in many rural households.

Willow withes were commonly employed in making commodious market baskets, covered clothes hampers, and the utilitarian Monday morning "wash baskets." Because of the slender willow strips (which like the oak strips had to be immersed in water for some time to make them sufficiently pliable to handle) considerable time and labor had to be expended in their creation. However, they were substantial almost beyond belief, and outlived many a generation of flimsy, factory-built receptacles. Willow baskets were much lighter in weight than the oaken variety, a fact which perhaps explains why they were so commonly used about the house.

Peculiar to the Dutchland are the rounded or vase-shaped straw receptacles once used for storing a winter's supply of *schnitz* (dried apples), or as repositories for feathers to be used later for pillows or featherbeds. These cavernous containers were sometimes more than two feet high and capable of holding more than a bushel. They usually had lids, few of which survive today. Of bulbous construction, they swelled toward the middle and then narrowed more or less gracefully toward the top. Some are frankly squatty, while others are as finely proportioned as any vase turned on the potter's wheel. The long, straight stems of oats or rye used in their construction are tightly confined by narrow wooden splints bound round and round the inch-thick bands of straw and cunningly interlaced with the splints of the preceding tier. A continuous rope of straw is used. Early beehives were constructed in essentially the same manner and of identical materials. With age and disuse the straw becomes rather brittle, but even so there are *schnitz* baskets now in service in their fourth or fifth generation. One large specimen commands an honored place in a country-home-in-the-city as a laundry hamper.

Similar in construction are the small Mennonite bread baskets, in whose clean straw freshly kneaded loaves of bread were placed to rise after the dough box had served its purpose in the baking preparations. Bread baskets are either circular or elongated, and usually only a few inches deep. As a rule they are so tightly woven that the non-initiated are apt to think that they are made of coils of rope. Most of them are so constructed that they will nest like mixing bowls; a few of them have a single handle by which they may be hung on the wall. Country children not so long ago thought of them simply as Easter-egg baskets, and perhaps such a use was a fitting reward after the visits of a neighborhood baker released the little straw coils from their purely ancillary duties in the kitchen. Nowadays, sponged lightly with dry suds and subsequently shellacked, they may perform a multitude of services in any room of the house.

Finally there is the delicate "Chinee" basket of raffia-like material, so ornamental that it need perform no actual service. It may or may not be true that these intricately woven little containers were imported from China, as some maintain. Certainly it is true that they are of exquisite workmanship. Pale in color, and with tops and sides lightly ornamented with painted flower clusters, they range in size from round ones no bigger than a silver half-dollar to specimens several inches deep and eight inches or more in length. Many of them have double handles, and tops which may be lifted by a projecting tab. It was probably a Victorian affectation that led to lining some of them with satin and to lacing ribbon through the interstices at the top when the construction permitted. They may be utilized for various purposes, according to their construction and condition, but why not do as their original owners did, and have them "just for pretty"?

Spatterware

No housewife would have the temerity to set her dining table with costly spatterware, that acme of Pennsylvania Dutch china, even if it were possible to assemble a complete set of one design. Still, no stone house would be complete without at least a few specimens judiciously disposed where they might do the most good, decoratively speaking. Spatter has been so widely collected of recent years, and so much has been added to collections that give every appearance of remaining as firm as Gibraltar, that the newcomer must be contented with picking up an occasional piece here and there.

Spatterware is a Staffordshire product made and decorated for the American trade. It is a rather heavy, soft-paste tableware, and its ornamentation is primitive and rather gaudy. We must suppose that it was shipped to this country in considerable quantity and in a marked variety of patterns, perhaps as early as the end of the eighteenth century, but more probably in the decades from 1800 to 1840. The actual process of spattering was a very simple one, and consisted of dipping a small sponge into any chosen color and then applying it more or less evenly in a series of dabs to the edge or to the entire surface of plate, cup, saucer, or other dish. This spattering in most cases served as a background or border for a design outlined in black and then filled in by hand with a brush dipped into color. The glaze was afterwards applied in the manner usual to chinaware.

Yet for all its simplicity and in spite of the fact that it was created outside America for a buying public presumed to be incapable of appreciating anything but bold colors and crude designs, it has all the appealing qualities of the folk art it is not. It was made expressly for the Pennsylvania Dutch, and although tentative consignments seem to have been sent to New England and perhaps to Virginia and points farther south, it remains to this day one of the two types of chinaware regarded everywhere as characteristically "Dutch."

For years the most widely collected design has been the peafowl, perhaps because the early collectors who gave impetus to the movement found it most plentiful. The Adams peafowl (that is, the fowl characteristic of dishes bearing the Adams pottery imprint on the bottom) is generally regarded as most desirable. A typical Adams peafowl may be described as a bird standing rather erect on legs and feet which are simply black lines. The body consists of a central oval or ellipse, from which two lines continue gracefully upward to converge at the head. Another line is extended backward to the top of the long tail. The head itself consists of a disproportionately small circle with a single dot in the middle for an eye. The bird is usually shown looking over its back, the sharp beak marking the beginning of a sweeping curve from beak to tail. The head bears a tuft of three feathers; two wavy black lines of doubtful function spring from the mid-back. The spreading tail of the bird is filled in closely with brush strokes of color below the back-line, but without any outlined boundary below. As in the case of most spatter peafowl, the plumage is in three colors. A fourteen-sided nine-inch plate spattered in pink, for example, boasts a bird with purple breast and neck, a green body and red tail and crest. Other color combinations are blue, yellow, and red; red, yellow, and green; and blue, yellow, and green.

Peafowls are to be found on almost all the pieces which compose a dinner set: plates, cups, saucers, bowls, soup plates, platters, and pitchers. Rare here as in any design are cup plates, sauce dishes, gravy boats, and vegetable dishes.

While the Adams birds are usually drawn and colored with more skill than those on unmarked pottery, they are not the only ones considered collectible, at least if salability may be counted as the criterion. Not much spatter is identifiable as to its maker. Considerable research has revealed impressions of "B & T"; "Tunstall"; "Stoneware B & T"; and finally "B. T. Troutbeck, Tunst.," indicating with some certainty that the different colors and designs showing these markings were all made at the same place.

After the peafowl the schoolhouse design seems to be most widely sought. Whether the little box-like building is really a schoolhouse, whether it is merely a shed, as some specimens would seem to indicate, or whether it is a log cabin reminiscent of the Harrison presidential campaign of 1840, as has been suggested, will probably puzzle collectors for a long time to come. Propounders of the schoolhouse theory, who base their claims principally on the fact that the building is little and red, and therefore a schoolhouse, have no argument left when confronted with a little *blue* house. Others maintain that before the Harrison campaign was, the spatter cabin was. But whatever the origin of the house it looks very well on spatter, and a complete set of it could command a sum which would go far toward buying a stone house or sending a boy through college. The house, whether red or blue, usually boasts a chimney, a door, and three windows, two at the side and one above the door. There is usually a more or less nebulous spatter tree near by, and occasionally a grass plot. The roof is yellow, the windows and doors white.

The basic color, that is, the actual sponged color of spatterware, has much to do with its choiceness. Yellow is by far the rarest, and therefore most highly prized. After that green is hardest to find, although one may accumulate a dozen pieces of it without ever running down a piece of yellow. Even long-established dealers have been known to admit that they have never seen a piece of yellow. After these two, in no particular order, pink, red, and blue make their claims. Purple is not too highly thought of, according to some dealers, although it commands a higher price than blue. Brown and black, although desirable, are less attractive than most of the others. Colors are often found in combination. Peafowl cups and saucers, the background of which consists of approximately even areas of soft red, purple, and blue, are by no means unknown. A curious fact about this variegated ware seems to be that while the cup-peafowl is blue, yellow, and red, the saucer-bird is blue, yellow, and green. Alternating stripes of pink and green with no other decoration are now and then found on platters, small bowls, and plates. Pitchers and sugar bowls in blue and yellow are not too uncommon, and occasionally such astounding combinations as brown and black, or blue, purple, and black are to be found.

The fact that only cups and saucers, or only plates are mentioned in connection with any one pattern or color does not mean that other pieces are spurious; far from it. The chances are that any lone survivor was once a member of a complete dinner set, all the remaining pieces of which have been broken or carried elsewhere. Spatterware was plentiful and cheap at one time, and therefore not so highly valued that it was handled with great care. Cheap? Not long ago a dealer who has spent a small fortune in buying peafowl and schoolhouses displayed a pile of a dozen red schoolhouse plates in proof condition. She named the fabulous sum for which she had bought them back from a millionaire collector to whom she had sold them years before. Then came the surprise. "Turn them over," said she. And on the bottom of each, scrawled in the black crayon of a century ago appeared the unbelievable legend: "9¢."

Peafowl and schoolhouses are, at that, by no means the rarest of the patterns. Probably the most elusive of all is the parrot, who perches precariously on a thin black twig, his green and red body and fancy top knot displayed to perfection while he eyes the visitor knowingly. A parrot, from the point of view of rarity, may be the gem of any collection. Not long ago, while the purchaser held his breath at his good fortune, a pair of parrots on a tall, beautifully sloping jar came to him because the dealer, apparently having no previous experience with them, congratulated herself on getting rid of birds that were not peafowls! This vase, whether intended for celery, spoons, or something entirely different, seems to be unique in the spatter confraternity.

Another hard-to-find pattern is the dove, whose blue, yellow, and white body is set against a background of what may be called olive branches. For some reason the dove seems to have an affinity for pink spatter, though purple and perhaps other colors are also known. The windmill, the cannon, and the sailboat are found rarely, so rarely, in fact, that there seems to be little point in more than mentioning them.

A well-known and attractive design is the so-called open tulip, a four-inch, six-petaled flower in red, blue, and white. Tiny sprays of green are outlined between the petals. These tulips are oftenest found on red and on blue spatter, with now and then a deep yellow or purple. It would not be impossible, with diligence and good fortune, to assemble a tea set in this design, since plates, cups and saucers, creamers and sugar bowls, and tea pots may all be found. That the task is not too easy of accomplishment may be attested by the plight of one collector who, having accumulated five open tulip blue plates in two weeks, has hunted unsuccessfully for seven years to find a sixth. Profile tulips and several variants of the tulip pattern are less interesting and spectacular than the open variety, which for some strange reason is also known as the sunflower!

The rooster is a good pattern. So is the Adams rose, which shows to equal advantage on yellow or brown. The acorn is well drawn, and not so highly sought after but that one may buy good specimens reasonably. Another in this category is the thistle design, which bears a somewhat unfortunate resemblance to a shaving brush, but which is a good pattern for all that. It has also been called the carnation. The star design is very attractive; the beehive less so.

One pattern is known as New England spatter for the simple reason that it is oftenest found in New England. Complete tea sets of this have been offered for sale in the past. The spatter is always blue. A central gray, tower-like object with two red dots is flanked by black cylindrical projections. A green spatter tree springs nonchalantly out of one of these, and other trees stand near by. Birds wing away in the middle distance. The enigma as to just what is represented is not solved by the fact that one school of thought maintains that it is a steamboat going down on the rocks, and another that it is a baronial castle. The most important piece known to the writer is an eight-inch covered vegetable dish. Plates, cups, and saucers are not highly regarded unless in absolutely proof condition. Another puzzling design is one which is known to the trade as the wigwam, or the Indian village. A unit of two slanting cylinders is flanked on each side by two conical sections which might be Indian tepees. The trees and birds of the New England spatter appear again here. The design is over-large for the plate (the only article commonly found); yet a very attractive effect can

SPATTERWARE PATTERNS

PINE CHEST

be secured by standing a row of them, one each of various colors, on a plate rail or an open dresser. They appear at their best when seen from a distance.

Still other patterns may be found, some appealing, some merely curious, some gauche. A four-petaled clear blue flower on brown spatter, bluebells, harebells, winter berries, plaid, and spatter dabs that are just dabs and no more—all these find buyers.

Some spatter was made in America, but it is inferior to the Staffordshire product in color, and the texture, while softer to the touch, is that of late ware, perhaps as late as the 1860's. Chocolate pots, children's "play dishes," and cups and saucers, all in a muddy, all-over blue belong to this group. Another late type of spatter, hardly worthy of the name, seems to consist principally of overlapping rings of color strewn about the surface of the plate, the center of which contains a discouraged-looking red and white tulip. None of the Staffordshire designs appear on the American spatter.

Cups, of course, are handleless, but now and then an authentic miniature with a handle is found, and occasionally a child's drinking mug with a handle.

As already indicated, some pieces are harder to find than others, and oddities are treasured. Cup plates, which held the cup while tea was leisurely sipped from the deep saucer, rate as scarce. So do butter chips and salt and pepper cellars. Milk bowls and porridge bowls, which contain about two cupfuls of liquid and are shaped exactly like cups, are seen now and then. Sugar bowls are plentiful, as are tea pots and pitchers, but other bowls, particularly covered ones, are not often found. Lids of whatever kind are scarcer than the vessels they should cover. Vegetable dishes are not often to be had, and sauce dishes are practically non-existent. Now and then a large ewer and bowl are seen at shows. The beginner in spatter would do well to start with plates, cups, and saucers.

An interesting variant in spatterware is that in which one of the transfer designs used on historical Staffordshire ware appears as the central motif. Edges of such dishes commonly have a deep border of blue, and, more rarely, pink. Similarly, a patriotic design of shield and stars is come upon now and then. A "set" of about forty pieces was offered for sale a few years ago.

Spatter has been reproduced, but not in a wide variety of colors or patterns. The only one which might fool the amateur seems to be a round vegetable dish with a spurious Adams rose in the center. Border colors detected thus far seem to be confined to blue, red, and green. In a different design, units consisting of a tea pot, tea plates, cups and saucers are being handled in the five and ten cent stores. The spattered edges are in red, and are well done, but the bold floral design is nothing known to real spatter. For the householder who does not wish to spend the time or money involved in accumulating the real thing, this imitation ware has its merits. It is colorful, akin in spirit and in execution to the genuine article, and not too precious to use.

If the beginner is confronted by a piece the authenticity of which seems questionable, he may apply the following reasonably accurate test: Unglazed spatterware, after being decorated and dried, was stacked in piles for firing, thin triangular platforms being placed in the bottom of each dish to keep its neighbor from nestling too snugly. As a result, three unglazed dots about the size of the head of a large pin appear in almost all flatware pieces, at the places where the points of the triangle rested. The presence of these spots has been a pretty safe sign for the beginner in the past, and will continue to be so until a clever counterfeiter, impressed by market prices, begins to use the same method.

Gaudy Dutch and Other China

FULLY as typical of the Dutchland counties as spatterware is its even more colorful Staffordshire companion, Gaudy Dutch. Whereas spatterware is heavy and its decorations not far removed from the primitive, Gaudy Dutch is light in weight and makes some pretension to elegance. It too was a product aimed at the American market, and seems never to have gone far beyond the fan-shaped region spreading out northward and westward from Philadelphia. Cherished for its vivid coloring, bold designs, and general appearance of fragility, it undoubtedly appeared oftener behind glass doors than on the dinner table, though occasional pieces bear all the tokens of hard use.

Gaudy Dutch designs bear a strong resemblance to one another, so strong, in fact, that to the beginner the points of differentiation seem trivial. The decorations are freehand, on a white background, the colors almost invariably being deep blue, iron red, apple green, clear pink, and clear yellow. Cobalt blue is used for edges or borders on plates and saucers, in a sense framing the lush leaf and floral decorations which appear as though they might otherwise get out of bounds.

Gaudy Dutch is older than spatterware, having come from England during the period of about 1785 to 1815. Its designs are not of English origin but, as has been now and then suggested in the case of spatterware, may be traced back to a much more ancient origin, in this case to China. Of course, the same thing is true of a great deal of other English pottery, from Lowestoft to willowware. In this instance, though, some of the fineness of the Chinese motifs has been sacrificed purely for vividness in color. There are those who think otherwise, but a really sizable collection of Gaudy Dutch is so overpowering that at close range it is apt to become confused and meaningless. Displayed against a plain background where it can first be viewed from a distance, it achieves a distinction it does not command close up.

The names of the various designs are neither inspired nor, in some cases, particularly accurate, but appear to have been bestowed by hard-pressed antique dealers. There is additional confusion because of individual and arbitrary attempts to re-christen patterns already known by different names in another locality. Perhaps the Vase or Flower Pot is most unmistakable.

In this an urn or vase of blue occupies the center of the field with a pink six-petaled rose above it, and "buds" and green leaves spreading out to the border.   The vase, ornate but not shapely, rests on a blue ground from which spring tufts of foliage.   The border in this design is floral in nature and is customarily divided into eight sections separated by narrow blue bands. It has been suggested that the rose, which is out of all proportion to the size of the vase, replaces a lotus used originally in real Chinese ware.

Another design, and one of the best, is the Indian War Bonnet, so called because of its central arrangement of blue feathers, one above and four below the headband, as worn in the original by the chieftain bent on trouble.   The uppermost feather actually appears to be a leaf, but is referred to as a feather out of courtesy.   A many-petaled rosaceous flower almost fills the upper surface of the headband not occupied by this blue plume.   Smaller flowers, buds, and leaves fill the remaining space with more restraint than in the case of the Vase design, and perhaps for that reason the War Bonnet is more effective.   The border is divided into sections separated by blue bands, as is true of the Oyster design, in which a rose, not an oyster, dominates the scene.   The appellation of "Oyster" comes from the fact that a geometrically shaped figure, several inches long and approximating the form of an oyster shell in profile, is boldly superimposed upon the floral pattern, with an unfortunate disregard of artistic effect.

The Butterfly, with its rusty-red wings, is aptly designated, but why the Dove should have been so called remains something of a mystery.   Its narrow border gives it an air of distinction, however.   The Grape pattern may have been thus labeled from the fact that the many-petaled flower of its central figure somewhat suggests a bunch of bright pink grapes, or even because the leaf below it is not unlike that of the grape.   The dahlia in the pattern of the same name is accurate enough to be recognizable, at least after one has had it pointed out to him.   The floral composition here is neat, but the pattern commands a considerably lower market price than the highly desirable War Bonnet.   Another flower pattern is named for the sunflower, which it does not even remotely resemble.   The Carnation and the Double Rose designs are quite similar and are often confused.   Perhaps the Single Rose displays the most admirable composition, with its heavy blue border, brownish-red rim, and tiny parallel stripes (where there should be no stripes!) in the heart of the flower.

Perhaps there is little point in trying to discriminate among these closely related patterns, for none seems to possess a merit which would place it head and shoulders above any other.   If any may be suggested as most popular the War Bonnet, with its historical implications, is outstanding, though all are desirable.   Prices vary according to the condition of the piece rather than the design, even a disputed pattern called No-name by general consent being able to command an immediate sale at what must be regarded as a fancy price. Gaudy Dutch is practically always unmarked as to place of origin, although the name Riley, presumably that of a Burslem potter of about 1800, is infrequently found.

For the householder who would acquire a single piece, a plate to hang on the wall for purely ornamental purposes would be a good choice. A unit of matching plate, saucer, and handleless cup would be a good buy. A tea set, consisting of tea pot, hot water pot, sugar bowl, creamer, plates, cups, and saucers would be a worthy goal, even if one had to fill in with pieces of varying designs. There are several things the beginner ought to do before making a single purchase, however. He should visit a collection, whether in a museum or a private home, and try to memorize its general appearance, noting the strong colors, with the predominant pinks and blues. He should take cognizance of the borders, with their variations in width, design, and depth of color. Incidentally, one way of assembling a collection of Gaudy Dutch is to choose it by its distinctive border. He should note the flatness of the plates and the marked concavity of the saucers. Thus equipped he should be able to avoid some of the pitfalls of the ill-informed buyer who sometimes is compelled to make a quick decision at a country auction, only to regret it later.

Among other tablewares more or less typical of Pennsylvania is Gaudy Welsh, a thin porcelain oftenest found in tea sets or in miniatures. The background in a typical plate is about equally divided between white and a deep purple with luster decoration. There are three areas of purple, roughly triangular in shape, on a white field which bears a wild-rose-like flower in the center with three tulips and sprays of greenery near the edge. Flower colors range from yellow to orange. The straight-sided cups have handles and short feet. Purely for its decorative merits this type of chinaware has no very high rating; as a variant of lusterware or as showing a remote kinship with Gaudy Dutch (if only in name) it calls for some notice.

Roseware, widely known but hard to find, has an appeal all of its own, perhaps because the person who cares enough for it to make a single purchase will wish to keep on buying every good piece that comes his way. It is undeniable that sizable collections, perhaps because of the chaste simplicity of the design, show to better advantage than small ones. The red Adams rose probably has the greatest artistic merit and can be found in all the pieces needed for a dinner service, provided of course that one is willing to spend the necessary time and money. This Adams rose, so called because it usually bears the name Adam impressed on the back of each piece, is a free-hand, under-glaze representation of the full-blown flower in clear red. Brush strokes carry the color up the sides of the flower, represented in profile, and down from the top, leaving an inner portion in clear white. Attractive sprays of green leaves comprise the rest of the decoration. A plate contains the design as a border, two roses being shown, one at each side. A central sprig of green completes it. Plates are usually deckle edged.

The King's Rose design is less attractive, although it has its devotees. It is subject to considerable variation, especially in the borders, which frequently approximate those of Gaudy Dutch plates. Its principal characteristic is its orange-colored flower, which dominates minor details of vines and flowers from its position just off center. The Queen's Rose pattern is very similar, save that the rose is pink. Both differ from the Adams rose in that in flatware they are central motifs, whereas the Adams rose takes its place in a garlanded border. Variations of the rose pattern are occasionally found, and a related design, the strawberry, is both colorful and attractive.

Heavy stoneware with a pattern of moss rose makes a not unattractive collection, although the individual pieces are on the ponderous side. Pitchers, sugar bowls, batter jars, platters, and other massive articles have withstood the ravages of time better than the smaller pieces. Plates seem to be rather scarce, although once in a while a complete dinner service is offered for sale. The pink rosebuds in their misty greenery, when unfaded, are quite effective against the highly glazed white surface of this ware, but there is no reason to suppose that Pennsylvania was the only place where it was sold. It is of late manufacture, and presumably was widely distributed.

Another heavy ware was the plain, crimped-edge ironstone china of not much more than seventy-five years ago. The colored border, not more than a quarter inch in width, is generally in blue, but occasionally in green and rarely in red. Because of the many finer types of chinaware available, this utilitarian form has been but little collected. Still, it has an air of engaging rustic simplicity, and appeals particularly to those who are able to remember the days when its great platters held strawberries for sun-preserving or cut corn for drying.

Old gold-banded china is a good choice for those who wish for a setting that is simple and restrained, but at the same time distinctive. "Fruit" plates, bordered with a band in pink, blue, or other colors, and displaying a single fruit or a cluster as the central decoration, are nearly enough related in feeling to act as companion pieces for the gold-banded set.

Now and then a set of majolica is seen in a fine old Pennsylvania home. Potteries in Pennsylvania occasionally specialized in this ware, one of the popular designs being the shell-and-seaweed pattern. The colors include brown, pink, bluish green, and green, often in combination. Comparatively late, it is not often collected in any great quantity. A few specimens, notably leaf-shaped plates, are usually all that the average purchaser needs as examples of this branch of Pennsylvania Dutchiana.

An interesting and eminently collectible pattern for simple rooms and everyday use is the mottled pottery usually called Pennsylvania Bennington for want of a better name. The background ranges from white through cream, with a spattering of brown all but covering the surface, inside and out. It has only recently attracted much attention and should prove fairly easy to secure. Cups and saucers seem not to have been made, and but very few plates. Pitchers in various sizes ranging from small creamers to those whose capacity is several quarts are to be found, either plain or with raised floral designs. Tulips are considered desirable here, as in any Pennsylvania Dutch ornamentation. Bowls, large and small, are useful for fruit or for flowers. Platters, round, elliptical, or rectangular, are attractive and not too expensive. Oval side dishes, ranging from six to nine inches or more at their greatest length, are serviceable, the more so since vegetable dishes are sometimes hard to find in other wares. Shallow pie dishes are known; whorled sponge-cake dishes are very common.

Pennsylvania brownware of this sort was probably an adaptation for practical purposes of the somewhat finer New England Bennington pottery. An interesting variation apparently unknown to New England, though, is the blue and white ware, in form and shape conforming to the standard set by the brown. The blue is a clear tone ranging from sky blue to cobalt. For those who would create a table setting of old dishes, it may be suggested that blue-edged ironstone china and Pennsylvania blueware combine harmoniously. Brownware goes very well with spatter and has the added attraction of being available in pieces practically unobtainable in spatter— vegetable dishes, bowls large enough for mixed green salads, and great plates and platters commodious enough for cold cuts or hors d'oeuvres.

There are at least two other wares for which the Pennsylvania Dutch seemed to show a predilection, but which are to be found so generally in antique shops throughout the land that they can hardly be offered as truly representative of the Dutch country. One of them is the early Leeds pottery, which exists in a considerable variety of patterns and shapes. Those which especially merit the attention of the collector here are the occasional small plates, bowls, cups, and saucers which bear the peafowl design of spatterware. Whether these are actually earlier than spatter, the usual contention, or whether they are contemporary with it, is of less importance than the fact that they harmonize well with the spatter collection. Leeds peafowl are oftenest found in blue and orange or yellow and brown. Edges of plates are frequently closely crimped, and colored in green. The eagle-and-shield combination in a transfer pattern is a good choice, as is the "house" design. Besides the pieces mentioned above, there are tea pots, pitchers, sauce dishes, salt cellars, and possibly others, all of which would have to be listed as rarities.

The second ware mentioned as being found in Pennsylvania but not necessarily of it is Salopian. Although not particularly fine, in comparison with Dresden or Crown Derby, for instance, it is both delicate and fragile, a fact which probably explains its scarcity today. Its salient feature is its all-over transfer design, in colors predominantly brown, orange, gold, and blue. Among central motifs of bird, cabin, and deer, the deer is most highly prized, and is to be found on bowls, creamers, plates, cups, and saucers.

Obviously many choice wares not discussed here are to be found in Pennsylvania, perhaps in the very heart of the Dutch country, and to exclude any of them from consideration is to run the risk of appearing pedantic. Historical Staffordshire, luster, and others have their merits and their local collectors. They would do credit to any fine interior, and there is no reason why they should not be collected for the stone house. If one wishes to single out what may be called characteristic, however, let him start with some of the others first.

Glass

PROBABLY no phase of American craftsmanship has been explored more persistently or with more telling results than the subject of glassware. Still, it may not be amiss to add a footnote to the formidable total of findings, indicating how the seeker after a Pennsylvania Dutch atmosphere may make a practical application of the research that has already been done for him.

Inevitably thoughts of Stiegel glass and of the romantic "Baron" himself come to mind, and it certainly can do no one any harm to contemplate the delightful prospect of filling a corner cupboard with sparkling treasure picked up for a song at a country acution or two, somewhere remote in the Dutchland. A moment's contemplation will suffice, however, to realize that the likelihood of acquiring even a single piece without paying well for it is pathetically remote. Long ago most of the desirable pieces that could actually be authenticated (to say nothing of some that could not!) were permanently retired trom circulation.

There seems to be no doubt that vast quantities of glass of all kinds were produced by the tireless Stiegel and his many workers, and that this glassware traveled far from its Lancaster County place of origin. The trouble is, as far as the novice is concerned, that probably an equal or even a greater amount of glass of similar hue and form was produced in other places at a later time, in some cases by the same expert craftsmen who had worked for Stiegel. It may be that there are those who, out of long years of study and experience, are able to judge infallibly, but it is safe to assume that their number is very, very small. Genuine Stiegel is most safely accepted as such when its ownership, back to the time of the original acquisition, can be thoroughly documented. Because of the impossibility of such documentation except in rare cases, most reputable dealers will commit themselves no further than to say that any given piece is of the Stiegel type.

Nor does the mere fact of a "Stiegel-type" appellation assure the buyer that he is getting anything really desirable. There is modern Mexican glass on the market which has fooled more than one expert; there is "Stiegel" glass in museums that saw the light of day in Pennsylvania only after a long journey by express. Unless the purchaser has complete confidence in his dealer as well as in the dealer's probable accessibility to the real thing, he should turn a deaf ear to the siren call or take at least a fifty-fifty chance of being duped.

A good policy for the beginner is to examine department store Mexican glass, so similar to Stiegel in many ways.   Close study will reveal the variations of color, particularly in blue.   The appearance of the unground pontil mark; the air bubbles in the glass; the shape of the piece, especially in pitchers; the details of the handle; the degree of flare in the rim of the bowl; the actual weight of the tumbler; the ring of the wine glass when tapped—all these should be noted.   One may assume as the truth all he picks up here, for no one in his right mind would try to palm off Stiegel glass as Mexican. Next let the beginner seek out some of the enameled ware imported from Holland, Belgium, or Germany, such as perfume and medicine bottles, and study their coloring, the detail of the design, and the shape of the object. Again, it would be an exceedingly foolish dealer who would sell good Stiegel at the price he could get for these foreign pieces.   Then, when he has a workable knowledge of texture, color, size, and design as a background, the beginner may venture out to take his chances.

Glass of the Stiegel type is bought for display, not for use, and the selection of a desirable and a safe place in which to keep it should precede the purchase itself.   Individual tastes will dictate the choice of clear, colored, engraved, or enameled glass, but there would be a minimum of satisfaction, say, in standing a row of crystal clear wines on a glass shelf too narrow to accommodate the amethyst sugar bowl and blue pitcher which must perforce hide their brilliance in a dark cupboard.

Assuming that all these preliminaries have been considered, one may say that the neophyte is ready to sally forth, for instance, to an antique show. Perhaps he would like a set of clear wine glasses of the Stiegel type.   He will find them, looking much like western Pennsylvania, Ohio, or other wine glasses, with well-shaped bowls and sturdy stems, giving a clear, musical, ringing tone when held at the base and tapped lightly with a finger nail. Dealers sometimes have them by dozens, sometimes by ones and twos, oftener not at all.   Since this type of glass was hand blown, it is practically impossible to find exactly matching pieces.   If one wishes to try to match them, he may do it by the bowl, which ranges from the sharply vertical to the flatter and more capacious chalice; by the stem, which may be plain, "turned," tapering, or "cotton twist"; or by any combination of these.   The actual variations, as seen in important collections, seem to have been almost endless.

After the wines there are many other drinking glasses, including squatty rummers, plain, engraved, and enameled tumblers, large, tumbler-shaped engraved flip glasses and handled mugs.   Liquor bottles, especially pocket-sized bottles, perfume bottles, and still other bottles in clear, blue, amethyst, green, and amber have been found.   Highly desirable are those in amethyst, particularly in the expanded diamond-daisy pattern.   Almost equally beautiful are those in blue, although there is a tremendous variation in blue tones. Green is not so good a color because it is rather pale and lifeless, but few collectors have ever turned it down on that account. Amber is rare in Stiegel.

Tableware was turned out in all but mass production in the years of 1765 to 1774, the time during which Stiegel operated his glass works. Sugar bowls and pitchers have survived in greater number than jelly dishes or mustard jars but there appears from the records to have been a glass receptacle for every conceivable household purpose. Decanters, sweetmeat jars, mortar and pestle for pulverizing sugar, candlesticks, bowls in many sizes and shapes, vases, cruets, gimmals, and still others are known to have been made. Appealing to many because it is comparatively easy to find is the footed salt dish, which conveys a first impression of a squat, stemless goblet, if one may call a goblet stemless. These salts are usually in Stiegel's beloved blue, but a cloudy green is not too uncommon.

Chemists' phials, physicians' bottles, inkwells, and window glass filled the needs of the growing country. Actually, Stiegel tried with every means at his command to make the Colonies independent of foreign importations, and to that end secured some of the most skilled glass workers in Europe, but no degree of homemade skill and no homemade product could compete with the charms of Continental ware, as eventually he was forced to realize.

As even the beginner would know, any piece of Stiegel glass might take its place as the gem of a glass collection. Still, assuming that the collector has somehow attained that delightful station at which he may pick and choose, there are some items that may be suggested as worthy of a first choice. The flat amethyst pocket flask, sturdy and with a sheared top, is one of these. Patterns were created by blowing the molten glass first into a mold, and then expanding it with the mold removed. "Squares" or diamonds were thus created in the glass, with a daisy pattern frequently added. Some flasks are paneled at the bottom, with the diamond-daisy pattern above. As a separate specimen of paneled glass, a rummer, either without or preferably with a tall cover, would be representative, as would a blue vase with broadly flaring top.

For a specimen of engraved glass, in which the lines of the design were cut by the copper-wheel-and-diamond method, the flip glass comes to mind. Favorite patterns were tulips or baskets of flowers. Enormous flip glasses with appropriate designs were sometimes made for presentation pieces, but they are nearly outside the realms of possibility for the collector. Lacking a flip glass, one would find an engraved wine glass a good choice. Enameled glass might be represented by a water tumbler or a mug. The enamel was applied freehand, the colors generally being rust-red, indigo, yellow, pale green, black, and white. The turkey pattern is a typically American adaptation of the bird forms used by Stiegel's European workmen. The steeple or castle pattern is also distinctive.

For decorative purposes there are other types of early glass which are almost as hard to authenticate. Glass was blown in New Jersey at least as early as 1739, when Caspar Wistar, a Philadelphia button merchant, turned his attention from brass to bottles. To Wistar goes the credit for being the first flint glass maker in the country, and for being the first successfully to use clear and colored glass in combination. In addition to window glass, bottles, and the usual objects of tableware, this Jersey glass includes the large flat glass bowls so popular among collectors in recent years, and the blown balls, incorrectly termed witch balls, which were used as covers for pitchers, bowls, and tall jars. Wistar glass has little to do with the Pennsylvania Dutch, but has a homemade charm that enables it to fit in anywhere with simple surroundings and décor.

Very early bottles, wherever they were made, were inclined to be long and slender or short and squatty. Physicians commonly used the latter type. Square-sided "French" bottles came in later, and by the middle of the 1800's there were bottles of many shapes with names and pictorial impressions molded in the glass. A good deal of the attractiveness of glass bottles was lost when hand blowing gave way to machine production, since no machine which produced the endearing lop-sidedness and irregularities of the hand blown ware would have been tolerated.

For the small collector who is less interested in the authenticity of the article than in its attractive shape and color, a glass shelf in a sunny spot is recommended. If small windows flank one's front door they are an ideal place for colorful bits secured at modest prices. A dining room or living room or study window may be spanned by shelves for the same purpose. Aside from an arrangement that is obviously no more than a frank miscellany, there are several angles from which one may work. One collector will perhaps wish to display only blown glass, while another will desire only one basic color with its variations. Whereas a third is interested only in hats or slippers, still another tries to collect as many different colors as he can. At any rate pottery and china ought to be excluded for the best results, but any collection which displays an order that is apparent to the observer can probably be defended. The whole idea of these glass shelves is of modern origin, and if such arrangements can be used with telling results in Connecticut or on Cape Cod there seems to be no reason why the deep windows of the Pennsylvania stone house should not be used in the same way.

One type of glassware that has often been overlooked by collectors is the bottle encased in wickerware or basketry to increase its length of life. Basketry weaving of this type was often a side industry among the women folk in the home of the professional basketmaker, and so excellent is the workmanship on many of these bottles that one is compelled to marvel at it. Pocket flasks protected by wicker were given a lease of life they could otherwise hardly have attained. Bottles of almost any size or shape may be found thus encased, some of the broad, flat ones making excellent bases for lamps. Vinegar, wine, cider, and molasses were stored in great glass carboys before wooden casks were to be had in many communities, and a basketwork encasement decreased the dangers attendant upon handling them. Ordinarily one would hesitate to remove the protecting sheath unless a sheared lip and a tantalizing gleam of blue or amethyst proved so alluring that he felt there must be something exceedingly worth while beneath it. As a matter of fact, many of the carboys still to be found were probably originally enclosed in willow withes or white oak which eventually rotted away in some dark cellar. Transformed to beauty by being filled with chemically colored water or used for lamps in a very large room, these giants now find in society an honored place they never enjoyed in their previous incarnation. A commercial establishment for encasing bottles in wicker once existed at Stroudsburg, Pennsylvania.

The vogue for pressed glass is just as strong in Pennsylvania as it is elsewhere in the country, and the hunting is just as good. Presumably this commodity was as widely bought in earlier days in the Dutch country as it was elsewhere. Its very ubiquity, however, which in no way decreases its appeal for the collector, denies it any particular status as typical or representative of the Pennsylvania Dutch. Yet there seems to be nothing to suggest as being better representative of Pennsylvania in the matter of table settings of glass.

Individual tastes of course will determine the pattern chosen, but a few suggestions may be made on the basis of what has been seen in rural Pennsylvania homes not yet despoiled by the professional antique picker. In our grandmothers' day in the Dutch country beaded grape seems to have enjoyed almost unrivaled popularity, perhaps because its squareness and beading gave it the charm of novelty. Green in particular was treasured. Sets of berry dishes in hobnail accompanied by their parent bowl, footed or short, found an honored place in many a household where canned fruit made its appearance. Woe to the luckless grandchild who broke one of these pieces, because of the currently accepted dictum, "*Wann selli all sin, kannsht du kenni meh kaafe*" ("You can't buy any more when they're gone!").

Tall pitchers in a design approximating the Baltimore pear, and in cherry and berry patterns which are variants of those listed in standard books on the subject, seem to have been all but universal. Daisy and button, clear and colored, was to be found in every household. Sawtooth has been observed, and cane and rose-in-snow are not uncommon. Peacock feather,

"101," and sprig still fill the top shelves in high cupboards, happily for the advancing generation of collectors.

Milk white glass enjoyed great popularity, and rare was the home that did not preserve the nesting hen that served as a container for store-bought mustard. If the home decorator of our times wishes to utilize this late ware for occasional bowls, plates, and what not, he will find excellent precedent for it in Pennsylvania. Indeed, so crowded with the familiar blue and white were the tops of bureaus and washstands in many country houses that visiting relatives must have been hard put to find a resting place for their traveling gear.

Pottery and Crockery

ONCE upon a time the fires of the great kilns of Montgomery and of Bucks counties burned night and day, in order that the housewife might have pots for her apple butter, dishes for her pies, and bowls for innumerable gastronomic triumphs. Now most of the kilns are cold, and the present generation of Pennsylvania Dutch homemakers would scoff at the idea of using the lowly redware of their ancestors. Perhaps it is just as well. Certainly the rural housewife who could with equanimity watch her offspring drink milk from a fifty-dollar mug or serve pie from a plate valued in the hundreds would cause jangled nerves among collectors. To be sure, not many of the myriad pottery forms have commanded such dizzy prices, but even the lowliest vessels have attained a status at which it would be prudent to withdraw them from everyday service.

The secret hope of every collector is that somewhere, some time he may stumble on a fine piece of sgraffito, the ultimate in Pennsylvania redware. Sgraffito means, literally, "scratched," a term which describes the process by which the design was applied to the object before it was glazed. Only a few special pieces enjoyed such decorations: those intended for display, for gifts, for formal presentation, or, in some cases, to show just what a man could do with clay when he put his mind to it. The sgraffito process was actually the second of three steps. In the first phase a thin paste of white clay called "slip" was applied evenly over the surface of the object to be decorated. After this the design was cut through the slip and into the redware below with a sharp-pointed instrument. Finally a glaze was applied. Sgraffito pieces sometimes had to go to the kiln twice, once when the actual baking of the clay took place and again after the liquid glaze had been added.

Pieces most commonly chosen for this test of the potter's artistic skill were those with an inviting expanse of flat surface, such as pie plates and platters, although jars, bowls, and mugs were by no means neglected. From the specimens that have survived, it would appear that pies were not actually baked in these plates, but must have been transferred from some lowlier vessel of similar shape. Sgraffito ware does not often have the oven-blackened undersurfaces of ordinary pie plates. Tall bowls for tobacco and for sugar, replete with incised floral patterns; slip-decorated shaving or barber basins; lattice-work jars or bowls, now and then with a bird for a finial and dated as early as 1791—all these tantalize the collector from their safe shelves in the museums.

Decorative devices followed the tastes of the potters themselves, and, as might be expected, tulips were an overwhelming Dutchland favorite.   In fact, one early writer on the subject uses the term "tulipware" for the whole category of sgraffito.   The degree of verisimilitude in the tulip representation depended largely on the skill of the artist and on whether he worked from the original or from one of the more or less fanciful designs to be found on fractur, but some of them are very fine indeed.   No accurate summary of all the designs has been made, one reason undoubtedly being that, since no two are alike, the only complete summary would be a listing of every object. While tulips were oftenest employed, other flowers were depicted also, among them the fuchsia.   Flower designs were sometimes of flowers only, but occasionally of flowers in a vase, or flowers and birds.   Moreover, the tulip appeared somewhere on the plate in the great majority of cases, without regard to whatever other design it might contain.

Among birds the eagle was popular, but parrots, peacocks, pelicans, and doves were represented, as well as some that might most safely be called just plain birds.   The fish was infrequently used as an ornamental device. Animals included rabbits, lions, deer, and horses.   Colonial horsemen in headlong charge are reminiscent of the days of the Revolution.   Foot soldiers, drummers, and fifers appeared, as well as men and women not engaged in warfare.

Not the least interesting feature of the more important sgraffito pieces is the fact that the potter often supplied his name, or even his name, address, and the date.   This custom was not so much a bid for the attention of posterity as it was an advertising device.   Since his wares were usually shipped to a general store for distribution, often in competition with others, it was but natural that he should wish to identify himself in connection with pieces of superior workmanship.   Again, after several months of work at the wheel, shaping enough ware to load the kiln, the potter would mark at least one special piece by which he could identify the degree of success of that particular burning.   We are told that most potters had a shelf at home on which these specimens were ranged for display.

Pieces intended for gifts or for ceremonial occasions frequently bore inscriptions in prose or in rhyme.   The customary practice was to set the inscription at the edge, where it could be read by turning the plate round and round.   Such inscriptions were oftenest in Pennsylvania German, but now and then in English.   In jocular vein, many of them verge on the risqué. A few are better not translated.

The pity of it is that so few ceremonial pieces are available to the collector of today; still it behooves every interested searcher to keep on the alert for such specimens as may, by some freak of chance, come within his ken.

Only slightly less interesting are those specimens of redware which have not been incised, but which are slip-decorated only. Two types of slipware are to be distinguished. The first of these was intended for commercial use, and, as might be expected, was simple enough not to make inordinate demands on the potter's time. When the "green" clay of the newly-shaped pie plate, for instance, had dried sufficiently so that it could be handled easily, liquid slip was allowed to trickle through quills at the bottom of a cup used for that purpose, wavy lines being drawn according to any pattern that pleased the potter's fancy. Before it was entirely dry this slip design was beaten into the clay so that it was flush with the rest of the surface. Glazing completed the process.

The second type of slipware was intended for ornamental purposes only, and the slip decorations were allowed to stand out in relief. Such ridges in a piece intended for household use would have been impractical, for they would have crumbled under everyday handling. It is in these pieces that the great variety of decoration is apparent. Ordinarily only a single quill was used in tracing dates, names, and markings of all kinds. A favorite device was to write the name of the recipient, when the object was intended for a gift, or to couple the names or initials of both giver and recipient. Not only pie plates but platters, bowls, and other dishes were thus decorated.

The colors of slip and sgraffito ware are essentially red and yellow, depending on the two fundamentals of potting clay and glaze. Baked, unglazed pieces emerged from the kiln a brick red, which deepened and mellowed with age and use so that some appear almost black. As stated before, the slip itself was ordinarily white clay, which heat turned to yellow. Patches of brown, green, and black in some pieces were due to coloring agents such as copper oxide or manganese. The glaze was usually red lead. Pie plates were glazed on the inner surface only, the liquid being applied by a paint brush. Hollow vessels were glazed on the inside by swirling the mixture around until it had reached every portion of the pot, the remainder then being poured out. Pieces glazed all over were simply dipped into a tub or vat of the glazing mixture.

Certainly every interior which makes any pretense of being Pennsylvania Dutch should have, lacking a piece of actual sgraffito, a piece or two of slipware. There are still enough of these in circulation that one may turn down specimens in less than fair condition. As might be expected, only pieces with the very simplest of decorations are commonly found, but even they are striking enough to demand attention, whether they be great flared milk pans or small pie plates.

The collector should view a too-perfect specimen with suspicion, since excellent reproductions are on the market. For one thing, there are a few potters still at work, turning out specimens with the same designs used by their ancestors. Usually all that is needed is a close examination of the piece, for the honest workmen have customarily supplied their names and the date on the bottom of each article. They are the first to decry the practice of those who attempt to age their wares artificially and sell them through unscrupulous or careless dealers.

A very real service for the modern decorator has been rendered by two different potters who copied old and rare designs for purchasers interested purely in the art of the ware. Jacob Medinger, often called "The Last of the Potters," was so successful with his sgraffito that now, little more than a decade after his demise, pieces known to be his command very good prices. Medinger, who was burned to death in 1931 by the flames of his own kiln, should not properly be called an imitator but rather a survivor, for he utilized the old tools and the traditional methods of the industry as his father before him had done. If in later years he yielded to the importunities of those who demanded reproductions of time-honored designs, at least he often dated his pieces, perhaps sometimes to the buyers' secret consternation.

Another pottery which has attracted wide attention in contemporary times is that of the Stahl brothers at Powder Valley. Like Medinger they "kicked the wheel" in the immemorial way of potters, and produced until very recently frank imitations of older pieces (but usually with their own name and date) along with everyday wares that still meet a local need. Flower pots, baked bean pots, sugar bowls and creamers and a variety of pie plates may be purchased very reasonably, as well as an occasional more pretentious sgraffito pie plate. As they admitted with mingled feelings of pride and regret, some of their things have had a habit of turning up in antique shops, but through no fault of their own.

For the average collector there is a wide variety from which to select, oftener in private homes, local auctions, and rural shops than at shows, because their moderate prices would hardly justify transporting them any great distance. Pieces from the old Bell pottery are in greater demand in some circles than those whose origin is unknown, their large bowls, tall jars, and heavy jardinieres displaying prominent streakings of brown, cream, and green under the blaze. These bold, random colorings are not for everybody, it must be admitted.

Among redware, pots ranging from small ones holding no more than a pint to those whose capacity is several gallons can be used with good effect. The smaller apple butter pots, dark red in color, glazed only on the inside, are good to hold flowers, or simply to stand in a deep window seat. Large sizes may be used for fruit dishes or for lamp bases. Some are capacious enough for waste baskets. Unless they are actually dirty they should not be scrubbed, for too vigorous work with a brush will destroy the patina which gives them much of their charm.

Vinegar and molasses jugs and articles intended for table use, such as sugar bowls and pitchers, were glazed both inside and outside. There is no reason why specimens with the glaze intact should not still be used for the original purpose, or at least put to some useful task. Rarities in shape and coloring will naturally come to rest on the fireplace mantel along with pieces of slipware and perhaps sgraffito. Jugs with either wide or narrow mouths make a worthwhile collection in themselves, as do covered bowls and jars. The colors range, according to the metallic coloring agent used under or with the glaze, from red through reddish brown, reddish black, and deep black.

Not all Pennsylvania pottery is in red. Some of the most striking pieces are the heavy gray stoneware jugs, pitchers, and churns decorated in blue. These are to be found in almost every community in the country, for potteries in New York, New England, New Jersey, and elsewhere turned them out in profusion, in addition to the Pennsylvania output. While the shapes are interesting in themselves, particularly in the case of wide-mouthed pitchers, the floral and bird decorations are their principal attraction. Tulips are a first choice, and not too hard to find. Tulips appear on flat, covered crocks which would hold a cake, cookies, or fruit with equal ease; on pitchers which according to their size would serve for milk, water, or other beverages; on churns which, deprived of their tops and paddles, might hold umbrellas, serve as a cool repository for milk delivered early in the morning, or do credit to a terrace in place of the too-common refugee from the roadside pottery market. A pair of them, planted with ivy, would lend dignity to the entrance of a house.

After tulips, blue birds, ranging from the competently drawn to the crudely amateurish, constitute the most popular motif. Birds are shown perching on branches, on nondescript bits of foliage or on nothing at all. Sometimes they are depicted in combination with flowers. Incised lines made by the thumb nail or by some pointed implement held stationary as the pot went round on the wheel give a finished appearance that is equally true of good articles in redware.

Still another division of pottery is that which has been called yellowware, the yellow color being due to the glaze. This almost purely utilitarian pottery comes in small storage pieces, butter crocks, pickle jars, and the like, and in pudding molds of various designs. Of these the ear of corn is usually most highly prized. One apparently unique yellowware specimen is a hanging salt box with an all-over spatter design, which brought exactly five cents at a recent country auction. This jar, about six inches in diameter and six deep, was potted with an upward projection at the back.   Before the piece had completely dried this projection was pierced so that the container could be hung upon a nail, presumably in a warm, dry place.

Among the more or less miscellaneous pieces which rejoice the heart of the collector are such rare items as "puzzle jugs," from which the bewildered novice finds it impossible to drink, as the liquid, traveling by devious routes, emerges at an apparently innocent and wholly unexpected opening.   Bulb or strawberry jars, which are specially constructed flower pots with side openings to accommodate bulbs or small plants, are more novel than decorative.   Colanders, once used in cheese making and for other household purposes, look well when filled with fruit or when holding a spreading fern or house plant.   Milk coolers, great bowls with a capacity of several gallons, are impressive on massive pieces of furniture.   Pudding and cake molds are attractive.   More or less of a rarity is the container which when filled with hot water served as a footwarmer.   Not of Pennsylvania origin but similar in feeling are the tall stone gin bottles imported from Holland.   The colors range from grayish yellow to deep buff.   They are particularly good as lamp bases, or, like any of the narrow-mouthed jugs, as candlesticks.

In addition to clay pieces which were formed on the wheel there is a profuse variety of diminutive hand-molded wares, largely ornamental. These will be discussed in a later chapter.

Painted Tin

THE gayly colored tinware of the Dutch country, like so much of the bright household gear of the region, stems from a European background, in this instance Wales. It probably came into being as an imitation or adaptation of Chinese lacquer work, taking on a new identity as new media were used for experimentation. Japanned ware, that is tin-plated sheets of iron thinly covered with varnish over which colored decoration was applied, was made at Pontypool in Wales before the end of the 1600's. In Pennsylvania it was produced during the first half of the nineteenth century, its many-colored birds and flowers endearing it to the hearts of the beauty-loving Pennsylvania Dutch. Similar wares, often of superior quality, were produced elsewhere, notably in Connecticut and Maine, but there seems to be a separate decorative trend in form and coloring peculiar to Pennsylvania. Presumably the work of highly skilled tinsmiths, these trays, boxes, and other objects are now lumped together under the general name of tôle, or Pennsylvania tôleware.

First in interest as in versatility are the painted trays which delight the amateur and connoisseur alike. A convenient classification for trays is by the edge employed, either straight or curved in what is known as the "Chippendale" manner after the lines employed by the great cabinetmaker. These Chippendale trays range in size from small ones about five by ten inches to those which measure eighteen by twenty-four and infrequently even larger. Trays of the better sort are reinforced by a heavy wire on the under side, the single sheet of which the tray is composed being neatly bent down over the wire at the edges. A few of the larger ones have cut out sections at the ends to enable the bearer to obtain a good grip. This happy circumstance is now a great convenience for the householder, who often wishes to display his purchase as he would a painting.

Chippendale edges seem to have been used principally on shallow trays. Straight edges, however, appear both on flat trays, large and small, and on deeper vessels known as apple or bread trays. The sides of the apple trays flare out at the top, some of them with swelling curves only at the ends, but others with graceful lateral projections as well. Now and then such a tray with a square base turns up, but most of them are oblong. Several oval-shaped dishes with lunette-shaped cut-outs in place of handles are known.

Basic colors range from the fairly common to the extremely rare in about the following order: black, brown-black, red, yellow, cream, blue, and green. This is true not only of trays but of other objects as well, with the reservation that cream and green seem to have been used only on trays. The matter of their basic color is a relatively important one, at least for the advanced collector. The beginner will usually be content at securing any tray with the original paint intact, the condition of the paint being at least the second most important consideration.

The choice of design will depend on the taste of the individual, but certain suggestions may be offered as a guide. Peacocks are not only truly representative of Dutch Pennsylvaniana but are at their best in full color on painted tin. An unusually fine peacock design is one that, in combination with a floral grouping, occupies practically all the flat surface of the tray. No two are identical, since the designs were freehand, but all are so similar that they must have been copied from the same pattern or from one another. The peacock is poised on a spray of greenery, looking forward or sometimes back over its shoulders. His head and neck are red, his wings red and blue, and his body blue and gold, usually with spots or mottlings of red. The long, sweeping tail is of plumes of creamy yellow, thinning out at the extremity to merge with the black background. The peacock's eye is sometimes outlined in black and gold, sometimes in gold only. The golden crest is raised, and frequently the bird appears to be screaming in anger. Those who find it hard to reconcile this brilliant creature with the actual *genus Pavo* contend that it possesses many of the characteristics of the bird of paradise. To the Dutchman and to the dealer, however, it is a peacock, and most collectors are content to let it go at that.

Below and to the right of the bird are two flowers, each measuring as much as two inches across in large trays. One appears to be a gorgeous red dahlia, the other a fringe-petaled bloom in cream and red or cream and blue, somewhat suggesting a great primrose. For some reason this latter bloom is always represented with two petals turned away from the observer, perhaps in a not-too-skillful attempt at indicating a deep flower cup. These flowers are surrounded by green rose leaves. Other lesser, lupine-like blooms in cream and red or cream and puce continue the design to the upper right, while violet-shaped blossoms cluster near the lower corners. A fine tracery of green vines and gilt arabesques fills in most of the remaining space. The deep borders of these trays are filled with conventionalized gilt leaf sprays. At the center of each of these there is a flower strongly suggesting dogwood, except for the fact that the petals spring from a red heart and vary in number from four to six. These border designs were stenciled in gilt.

This particular decorative pattern has been described in some detail because it represents what is probably the best in craftsmanship as well as

CHIPPENDALE TÔLE TRAYS

PUNCHED TIN PIE CUPBOARD

in coloring and proportion among the tôle trays. The peacock of the dahlias and primroses usually faces to the right. Now and then other peacocks are shown in different settings, but facing left. Perhaps "facing" is hardly the term, for in any pose the bird is apt to be peering back over his shoulders. One of the best of this second group is a bird which perches on a stone urn filled and flanked with brilliant flowers, among them some excellently drawn and colored fuchsias. He is a dyed-in-the-wool peacock, with his iridescent blue-green body, and with the "eye" markings on his tail clearly outlined. While the border is of the usual gilt type, the edge of the tray is unbound. This fuchsia-bird is probably Victorian, whereas the dahlia-peacock resembles the earlier bird of spatterware.

Other birds, too, are found on trays, some of them with highly improbable shapes and plumage, but all of them colorful and attractive. As a rule, the more exotic the bird, the greater is the array of flowers among which it poses. One indubitable bird-of-paradise hovers above a grouping of what may be poinsettia and harebells. The artist, perhaps with the thought in mind that nature abhors a vacuum, has filled in what would otherwise be a surrounding field of plain black, with concentric bandings of gilt and red paint. A final streak of red on the very rim serves as a binding for an unusually crowded border of blue-centered dogwood, pink-centered daisies, and leaves.

Some trays have a rhythmic pattern of comet-shaped brush marks in yellow as a border. Such markings are also characteristic of New England painted tin. It is not inconceivable that some of the early Connecticut pioneers who reached the Mahontongo Valley and other sections of rural Pennsylvania were responsible for this design, as for others that seem not to have any purely local counterpart. Some trays have large tomato-like decorations, the so-called love-apple motif. Some designs are good approximations of roses; others look more like chrysanthemums. Small elliptical- or octagonal-shaped trays with plain centers and flowered borders once may have served as bases for tea pots.

Good trays are becoming increasingly scarce, but there are still homes on the borders of the Dutchland that have them wrapped and laid away securely. Their value is well known, and their owners are usually in no hurry to part with them. Often they are in such good condition that it is obvious that they have never been used. Now and then dealers are able to secure them for favored customers willing to pay a round price. Unusual, perhaps unique, examples of this type recently noted include a thirty-inch ovoid form in deep cream with a luxurious gilt border and a cluster of brilliant red roses and buds as the central decoration. A cream-colored apple bowl and another in deep yellow banded in blue and gold-ochre were left undecorated at the bottom, as befits a vessel intended to be kept filled. A magnificent pair of small Chippendale-edged snuffer trays in dark green with gilt-leaved edging also falls in the category of rarities.

A word of caution is necessary at this point, about tinware that has been done over for the benefit of the unsuspecting. Some of this is offered openly as new work in an imitation of older designs. The thick paint, heavily laid on, and the brush work after the fashion of the painter in oils are characteristic. Other pieces are an imitation both in technique and in design, using genuinely old, undecorated, tin pieces. It is against these that the beginner must be on guard. As in the case of Stiegel glass, a good beginning is to purchase a small piece of the re-decorated or newly decorated tinware, with the intention of close study. Gift shops are now commonly stocking small articles of this type, and a few dollars so invested could not be better spent. Really old pieces are almost always crisscrossed by tiny age checks, not only in the background but in the designs. New work cannot duplicate these, although some pieces look pretty convincing. New pieces usually attempt to gild the lily by improving on the originals in some way. Frequently designs found only on choice bits of fractur turn up on boxes of rare yellow; common, battered tin candlesticks, newly be-flowered, rear their heads. Lamps, coffee pots, scoops, and metal containers in colors never known to the Dutchland are making their appearance in increasing numbers. Let the buyer beware!

While trays exercise a special fascination for many a collector, it does not follow that they are the only forms of tôleware worth buying; there are, indeed, collections of major importance which do not number a single tray. In the not-too-remote past, when the interest in Pennsylvania Dutch household effects had not yet become an obsession with the department stores, coffee pots were of all tôle articles the most desired. These, of course, were the "company" coffee pots which were carried to the Pennsylvania Dutch dinner table after the beverage had been brewed in some lowly vessel and then transferred to its more resplendent container. As in the case of important sgraffito plates, it is probable that really choice specimens were never used, but were kept at hand in an honored place for the ultra-important occasion that never arrived.

Coffee pots "for pretty" were ordinarily of black or brown-black japanned ware, and sported decorations of heavy globular flowers and green leaves. Some of the flowers are akin to the Adams rose of chinaware; others are mere daubs of strong color overlaid with contrasting markings to suggest flower petals. One typical example has the pomegranate boldly depicted, and others bear fruits suggesting the plum and the tomato. Occasionally no attempt at a realistic design is made, but an abstraction in which red, green, and yellow are prominent occupies either side of the pot. Pots in red are usually decorated in gilt with a leaf and fruit design, but red as a color is increasingly hard to find.

Coffee pots vary considerably in structural details. Some of the lids are topped by small brass knobs, while others have a little, tightly coiled strip of tin at the front to serve the same purpose. Some spouts are merely cylindrical, while others are jointed, gracefully curved, and notched at the ends for easy pouring. Handles may be merely straps of tin bent into semi-circular form, or may have a curved reinforcement on the under side for convenience in handling. The bottoms of some are flat, while others have a platform base. Something of a rarity is the side-pourer, said to have been used for chocolate.

Tea pots are low and squat and rather scarce. It is not improbable that the tall coffee pots, if they were used at all, may have been used for tea as well. However, the great variety of tea pots in stoneware and china, a much more satisfactory medium for this use, probably explains their scarcity in tin. One small elliptical-shaped one is about six inches tall. It has a straight spout and is closed at the top except for a small hinged "trapdoor" opening with a segment of rolled tin for a handle. Its decorations are four pomegranates with yellow, comet-shaped brush marks which pass for leaves. The "strainer," made by stamping circles out of the tin in the wall behind the base of the spout, is considerably smaller than the similar coffee pot strainers.

Tea caddies, ordinarily large enough for perhaps a half pound of tea but infrequently in giant sizes, seem to have persisted in actual use longer than most other tinware articles, for even now it is by no means uncommon to find them partly filled with ancient but authentic tea leaves. These canisters almost rate a collection in themselves, for while there is ordinarily little variation in size or shape they have a wide range of floral decoration. Tulips in deep pink-red are particularly good, as well as large six-petaled flowers. Pomegranates and other fruit designs are not uncommon.

The forms of ornamentation already listed are repeated on a wealth of small household vessels. Handled measuring cups range in size from gills to quarts. Covered sugar bowls about three inches high are matched by neat pitchers as well as by covered syrup jugs. Now and then a drinking cup made without a handle comes to light. Salt shakers and spice boxes in plain japanned ware are commonplace; decorated ones are rare. Hanging match cases are plentiful; desk sanders for use in lieu of blotting paper, less so. Decorated nutmeg graters are known, ingenious little cylinders which unjoint themselves and display a grater and a nutmeg compartment when the tightly-fitting cap is removed. One dealer has unearthed an elaborate and colorful device for warming a small quantity of milk, complete with a small kerosene lamp set into the base.

Cash or document boxes which according to tradition always accompanied the driver of the Dutchman's own Conestoga wagon range in size from tiny, play-size specimens to those twelve inches or even more in length and eight in height. Of sturdy construction and sometimes with their original locks still accompanying them, they bear evidence of hard use. Such boxes in red are considered especially desirable. Their decorations are less detailed than those of similar construction found in New England. A rare variation of this treasure chest is the oval pattern, thus far reported only in red. It stands a good ten inches high, and its super-imposed markings of faded green and yellow are undoubtedly more attractive now than they were when new.

Among miniature forms are the small treasure chests mentioned in the preceding paragraph, matching the larger pieces in design and coloring. A tiny covered "blicky" or tin pail in red with a single white daisy on one side is perhaps unique, as is a small yellow drinking cup with a red Adams rose. No doubt these are survivors from sets of toys which long ago met their fate at the hands of Pennsylvania Dutch children.

Whereas the whole family of painted tinware has its origin in the japanning trades of Pontypool and Usk, as has been noted earlier, it is significant of the enterprise of the Pennsylvania craftsman that when it suited him to do so he discarded European techniques and used his own. Some time, some place, an unknown workman decided to use just plain paint in direct contact with the tin, doing away with the hitherto indispensable lacquer. The result was apparently satisfying in his own generation, for lacquered and unlacquered vessels similar in design were created in apparently equal numbers. Merely painted surfaces, however, have a strong tendency to flake away under adverse conditions of dampness and frequent temperature changes. More than one rueful collector has found that regular ministrations of the dust cloth are out of the question if an unblemished surface is to be retained. Red-coated articles seem to be particularly susceptible to this crumbling process. It is not unreasonable to suppose that painting was a fairly late simplification of japanning and, from the collector's point of view, a not too satisfactory one.

In any event, the best thing to do with the tin collection is to give it an advantageous spot on a plate rail or in a corner cupboard, against a light background, and then refrain from the temptation of handling it too often.

Unpainted Tin

PLAIN tinware might seem at first blush to be a medium ill-suited for home decoration, but ingenious workmanship made a thing of beauty out of even this lowliest of metals.   The punched tin frames used for mirrors, the punched tin lantern and the more or less ornate panels used in pie cupboards have been mentioned in preceding chapters.   Of the same genre are coffee pots, made in the early years of the nineteenth century, so attractive that they need no apology whatsoever.   Unlike the more common japanned or painted vessels, these are frequently dated, the decade of the 1830's being most often represented.

Punched tin coffee pots make up in the minuteness of detail lavished upon them for the more showy coloring of their painted tôleware confreres. The punchwork appears on the outer surface as a design of raised dots, indicating that the design had been applied on the inner surface before the thin sheet was rolled to its proper shape and soldered.   The pots are made of many pieces in comparison with the few of painted tôleware.   Only one shape appears to have been used.   This was a geometrical construction of three conic sections—an inch-high base, on which rested a three-inch inverted segment, which in turn was topped by a nine-inch section.   Each of these was in two parts, fitting so exactly the section above and below that the soldering appears to form a continuous vertical line from top to bottom.   The handle and jointed spout were attached separately.   The dome-shaped lid was surmounted by a brass knob.   The capacity of such a pot is about two quarts.

The tulip was a favorite design.   In a representative specimen the upper section of the pot shows, on each side, an urn reminiscent of those used in the "Vase" pattern of Gaudy Dutch, or equally of those found on certain dower chests.   Springing from this urn are a well-shaped profile tulip and two open-petaled blossoms of comparable size.   Accompanying each flower are two leaves.   Two waved lines crossing at intervals of an inch are found on the "stand" or base of the pot, at the bottom of the upper section and at top and bottom of the middle section or "bowl."   Peacocks and conventionalized flower designs are found on some pots, the designs being identical, or nearly so, on each side.   When the name of the maker appears, it is

107

usually found on the handle.   "M. Uebele," "W. Shade" and "J. Ketterer" are three makers who cared enough about their work to affix their signatures. One unusual specimen is marked "J. Ketterer" on the handle and in addition bears on the body the initials "J. Y." and "H. Y.," presumably those of the owners.   Coffee pots of punched tin customarily have no strainer.   One wonders why there should be a strainer on a coffee pot anyway, since the openings found on the painted tôle vessels were too large to be of any use. Is it possible that those gaily bedizened creations were originally intended for *tea*, in spite of traditional tales to the contrary?

Pudding molds make attractive bowls for candy, nuts, or cigarettes, and are to be found in good enough condition that one may use them for molded desserts.   The sides are usually fluted, the panels carrying identical geometrical markings.   The principal design is the one at the bottom, which is deeply indented in the form of flowers, birds, and other patterns.   An ear of corn is a favorite motif.   Many of them are similar to the designs found on wooden butter molds.   These patterned molds are usually roughly oval in shape.   "Turk's head" molds, circular in form, are similar in shape to pottery sponge cake molds, their fluted surfaces spiraling upward from the bottom.   Turk's head dishes are also, though rarely, found in copper.

Match boxes in unpainted tin, or in tin with a protecting coat of plain red or black, are a late but useful adjunct to the kitchen or fireplace of the stone house.   One such box, "Patented in 1864," has a hollow cylindrical bed large enough to contain a good-sized handful of matches.   The cylinder is so balanced that its contents are completely concealed except when its lip of rolled tin is depressed.   The absent homeowner need have no fear of fires started by mice when matches are left in this container.

Mirrored comb cases of tin, with a trough spacious enough for a comb and brush, and a mirror large enough for at least an outline of one's face, continue to be used in many old homes.   In spite of claims of great antiquity by their owners they are very late, and only in rare cases attractive enough to merit a place with real antiques.

Of all the unadorned tinware products of the wandering artisans of the Dutchland, the cooky cutters of bygone days have most to commend them. Tradition has it that they were first intended as an aid to the busy housewife who, in her Christmas baking, wished to reproduce the forms of the star, the angels, the Holy Family, the manger, and the camel, the sheep, and other figures associated with the Nativity.   Certainly there are enough of these designs to lend strong support to the theory, but it might just as well be admitted that for every figure which could be identified with the Christmas scene there are a dozen which cannot.   One certain fact appears: these "fancy" cutters were used only at Christmas time, and still are used only at Christmas time in many a home throughout the length and breadth of the

Dutchland.   Perhaps on some day far in the past, in Switzerland or along the Rhine, a tinsmith, starting with stars and angels, decided to add patterns of more immediate interest for the sake of the youngsters of the house—the Christmas tree, the Santa Claus, and the wooden shoe.   If one pursues this line of reasoning he may account for later additions of dog, cat, or hen, on the ground that they too were familiar to children and would be recognized with delight when they made their appearance in edible form.   Indisputably, it is possible to trace a progression of designs down through the years, but it would be the part of discretion not to jump too hastily to the conclusion that cooky cutters necessarily have any religious significance.

The New England tinsmiths, we are told, created their wares of whatever sort at home, and then sent them out into the world on the peddler's cart for whatever they might command in cash or trade, usually the latter.   In the case of cooky cutters at least, the method in Pennsylvania seems to have been different.   The tinsmith created a set of designs, whether according to tradition, inspiration, or local taste, and with them visited homes lying within his chosen territory.   At one home, after he had satisfied the need for pails, funnels and the like, he might secure an order for his whole set of cutter designs, whereupon he would fashion them on the spot, using either his own left-over materials or others supplied by the thrifty householder. Numerous kitchen utensils, even candle sconces, bear mute evidence that they have been sacrificed for this purpose.   At another home he might find a goodly collection of tin hens, geese, ducks, and swans already in active service, whereupon he would be compelled to devise parrots, robins, eagles, and wild geese or lose a sale.   Now and then it would appear that the farmer himself, no tinsmith putting in his appearance, tried his hand at augmenting the family collection during his spare time, for not a few patterns are so clumsily executed that a tinsmith would hardly have risked his reputation with them.

One of these itinerant craftsmen, still remembered affectionately on the northern fringe of the Dutchland as "Old Nixon," in later years simply displayed his samples at country stores, where orders were taken for them. No signed specimens are known.   After all, they were only humble articles selling for a few pennies, and could have been no more than a by-product of the tinsmith's art.   Now and then an old home is broken up and among other things a string of cutters is put up for sale.   The auctioneer, prompted by a member of the family, will remark, "These were made by Old So-and-so," whereupon a few of the oldsters will nod their heads in recognition.

The cutters most serviceable to those who wish to carry on the good old tradition of Christmas baking are of moderate size, free from intricacies of design and equipped with good handles and "air holes" to ease the con- siderable chore of what the Pennsylvania Dutch housewife once called the "sticking-out" process. On the other hand, the most serviceable patterns from a utilitarian point of view are apt to be less interesting in an esthetic sense. The number so carefully treasured from one generation to another varied from a mere dozen or so to fifty or more. The size range would extend from a few baby cutters no more than an inch across to the twelve-inch horse or the great fifteen-inch gingerbread man. These outsize cutters are sometimes found almost like new, a fact which may be attributed to their impracticality in actual use. As one might expect, popular cutters of average size were used so often that the design indicated by the cutting edge shows through the tin backing, by sheer force of repeated pressure. Not infrequently cherished designs were traded back and forth among neighbors, and identifying names ("Sallie's cutter," "Ellie Hubner," etc.) were scratched on the back, presumably with the point of a needle.

Many patterns were equipped with two sets of cutting edges, the outer one actually cutting through the dough with the inner one making only a deep impression on the surface. For this incised imprint the tulip was exceedingly popular. A constantly recurring central motif of two or four tiny tulips with crimped edges and a spray of leaves gives interest to otherwise severely plain squares, oblongs, or circles. A heart was also frequently used. It must be admitted, however, that in actual modern practice the central design cannot be reproduced satisfactorily because of the insufficient depth of the auxiliary cutter. Evidently our forebears were fond of very thick cookies!

Most attractive among patterns bearing this inside cutting edge are those which utilize it as an essential rather than a superimposed part of the pattern. Leaves are given a striking degree of verisimilitude when the ribs are clearly outlined; an owl shape that is unique in itself is doubly enhanced by the addition of lines that indicate eyes and beak. Birds and barnyard fowl shown in profile emerge as individuals with the aid of wing and body markings, rather than as mere generic figures. Most helpful of all are the impressions which give definition to human figures by indicating eyes, nose, mouth, buttons, lines of kerchiefs, and ruffs. One of the designs of major historical importance, the Colonial horseback rider, emerges with remarkable clarity of detail from the welter of cutouts and incising edges used on the cutting board. Foot in stirrup, three-cornered hat on head with queue and ribbon behind it, this gentleman appears much like similar figures on sgraffito plates.

For the ardent collector it is not at all impossible to assemble in tin alone a satisfying reconstruction of rural times in Pennsylvania. Among historical figures are the Revolutionary soldier, William Penn with a gigantic peace pipe, the Indian in various poses, and the Indian maiden in buckskin. These give way in later times to the Mennonite-garbed woman, the stocky farmer, the Forty-niner, Uncle Sam in heroic proportions, and women in a whole succession of period costumes up to the puffed-sleeve era. Comic representations are frequent. Startled women with hands upraised, men grotesquely corpulent or extremely emaciated, figures brandishing fists or in unconventional poses, preachers in hortatory mood—all these attest to a robust sense of humor and a vigorous creative capacity in their makers. Dwarfs, baseball players, and dandies in tail coats came along in later years.

A full complement of domestic animals may be re-created in this early tinware: horses, standing, trotting, galloping, or doing circus stunts, and in a great variety of sizes; sheep in a design peculiarly Pennsylvania Dutch; goats; an occasional calf, but curiously enough no full-grown cow; pigs; donkeys; cats; and dogs ranging from shepherds and Saint Bernards to dachshunds.

Wild animals are by no means slighted, whether of local origin or copied from picture books or possibly the circus. There are rabbits done with great fidelity, deer, bear, wolves, skunks, foxes, squirrels, beavers, and still others. Lions are fairly numerous; camels and hippopotami are rare; a large and very realistic elephant seems to be unique. A whale two inches long vies in interest with a life-sized mouse. Barnyard fowl range from the common rooster, hen, duck, and goose to the scarcer turkey, guinea hen, peacock, and pigeon, and the exotic swan and Cornish game fowl. Wild birds in unidentifiable shapes are of less interest than robins, wild ducks, swallows, the parrots of fractur, an occasional magnificent eagle, and the unique owl previously mentioned. Judged by the composition of the tin and the nature of the design, parrots seem to have been the earliest of the tinsmith's birds.

Trees, leaves in considerable variety, and flowers would make a worthwhile collection in themselves. The tulip of course is the prime favorite, but because of that fact it is difficult to secure in good condition. The daffodil design and the thistle of spatterware occur now and then, but less frequently than flowers of conventionalized shapes. Among fruits only the pear, with its distinctive shape, seems to have been represented. A sheaf of wheat is reminiscent of similar patterns on wooden butter molds; a cluster of palm leaves with pendant fruits seems to be the only one of its kind.

A diversified array of household and other objects bears evidence that distinctive shapes of whatever sort came as grist to the tinsmith's mill. Boots and shoes, tobacco pipes, top hats, and bow ties; wheelbarrows and axes; clothes pins, bottles, pitchers and bowls; guns, pistols, and daggers; fiddles of various sizes; four-leaved clovers; keystones; half-moons and stars and still others are as appealing now as they were a century ago. Among them the flattish, round-lobed heart so characteristic of Dutch Pennsylvania appears again and again.

Occasional oddities, not to say rarities, delight the heart of the collector. Among these are the "double" designs in which a cutting edge is soldered to each surface of the tin backing. One such specimen has a bird on one side and a fish on the other; another has two conventionalized designs. Of more than passing interest is a wheel-like contrivance of four spokes, each of which contains a different geometric design at its end. A closed flour container two inches in diameter and four in length performs yeoman service by being equipped with a tin nutmeg pocket, a small grater, and three different cooky patterns. Of them all, the nearest approach to mass production is attained by a set of revolving blades attached to a long handle by means of a central connecting shaft. With this gadget it was possible to turn out little oblong cakes in almost no time.

Some cooky cutter collectors wish to put their finds to work, and there seems to be no reason why that should not be the case, as they are usually quite sturdy. Such minor operations as sterilizing them and applying a thin trickle of liquid solder to loose edges are recommended well in advance of baking day. Other collectors wish to utilize the shapes in more dramatic fashion. To this end the open shelves of a Welsh dresser may be requisitioned, or better yet a specially built wall frame with as many narrow shelves as are necessary. To display a really large collection (and there is at least one that numbers five hundred different designs) an entire side or end of a room would have to be fitted up. A frieze of cutters may be used for the walls of a play room or tap room, or the designs may be transferred to painted walls or to linen with better effect than commercially prepared stencils.

For a room in which unpainted tin pieces perform a decorative service, early tin candlesticks may be useful. They may be had in tall or low forms, either with or without handles. Unless they are of notably good design or are in unusually fine condition they should be used with restraint, as old tin unrelieved by signs of good workmanship is usually dingy in appearance. Candlesticks intended for wall use, particularly those having high sconce backs which flare forward slightly at the top to form a protective hood, are a good choice. The tray at the bottom of a representative specimen is capacious enough to take care of a pair of snuffers and a box of safety matches. They are intended to be hung on a nail, but are so light that they may be secured with a strong thumb tack. While they seem not to have been painted originally, protecting coats of black have sometimes been applied in later years. Such paint is easily removed by lye or a commercial varnish remover.

Early and attractive are the so-called mirror sconces, the circular shape of which is made up of mirrored surfaces placed together in small geometric sections. These reflectors are decorative either with or without candles.

A rarity in tin, and one which would be of actual use only in a very large room, is a great chandelier, circular in shape, originally intended for use in a meeting hall. There are two tiers of individual candle holders, severely plain in design. Another relic of earlier days is the handmade tin rack used in country Moravian churches at the traditional Christmas candle-light service. Such a creation seems to have been a product of purely local ingenuity, and could serve no purpose in the home except as a sentimental reminder of an appealing custom.

Wrought-iron candle stands of floor length, while not so numerous as they were in New England, are encountered now and then, and are useful in places where the usual short candlestick would not serve. Candle molds can be bought at almost bargain prices, the customary drawback to their purchase being that most persons do not know what to do with them. One possibility is to use them as a convenient storage-place for candles, assuming that the candles are of the right size and shape. If a punched tin lantern is used in conjunction with tin candlesticks, a mold might form part of a decorative grouping on its own artistic merit. There are also oblong candle boxes of pierced tin to be found.

Among a miscellany of unadorned tin objects which might be of interest to the antique shop explorer, the tin nursing bottle of a century ago commands attention. This amazing device, which may have contained half a pint or more of milk, was shaped somewhat like a small coffee pot with a tight cover, but with a spout standing out at right angles to the body. The end of the spout had a rounded mouthpiece, by the aid of which the infant could draw milk up through a slender tin tube which just cleared the bottom of the vessel on the inside. Apparently the only way in which the contrivance could be cleansed was to immerse it in boiling water and hope for the best.

Carved Wood

THE same urge which impelled the Pennsylvania Dutchman to paint his tinware with roses and tulips led him to try his hand at seeing what he could do with a sharp knife and a piece of wood. Sometimes the result was mere whittling, but oftener than not it had a touch of artistry which lifted it above the commonplace. From the simplest heart-shaped cut-out which formed the thumb-hole of a cabbage cutter to the lifelike and minutely carved eagle there is a distinctive quality which may stem from the toy carvings of Switzerland and the Rhineland, but which has purely local adaptations.

Best known to collectors are the works of the almost legendary Wilhelm Schimmel who, according to tradition, tramped about central Pennsylvania after the Civil War, carving toy figures for a precarious livelihood. At times, in payment for food or drink or lodging, he created the now realistic, now grotesque figures which posterity has honored with his name. Perhaps they were only the products of idle moments, sold during periods of wanderlust, but it has been claimed that they represented his sole means of livelihood. Whatever their reason for being, they come as near to the folk art feeling as anything Pennsylvania can produce.

Only a few years ago it was popularly supposed that practically all of the Schimmel figures in existence were in the hands of two dealer-collectors whose interests lay essentially in the field of primitives. Gradually others came to light and finally one of the dealers, perhaps deciding that it was useless to try to corner the market, offered her collection for sale. At about the same time a little-known private collection came into the hands of a third dealer, with the result that the average individual may now acquire a piece or two without much difficulty.

This third collection, conceivably the most important one of them all, caused no end of embarrassment to its owner in the remote village in which she lived. Eccentric that she was, she kept her treasures in an ancient and disreputable flour sack which hung on a nail in her untidy living quarters over a general store. She was fond of talking about them, and would insist on showing them to people who had no interest in them. As long as she let it go at that she was regarded as harmless, but when she announced locally that the collection could be bought for what seemed to the non-initiate a purely astronomical figure, she was dubbed insane and treated accordingly. She realized that the local gentry would not take her word for it if she did claim a successful sale. The upshot of it was that she tried to disperse the collection farther afield, but always lost heart at the crucial moment and finally died with it still on her hands. Almost immediately it was bought at a figure which would have vindicated her in the eyes of her neighbors.

Among the naïve objects which go by the name of Schimmel pieces, the eagles are outstanding. These are fierce-looking creatures, seemingly inspired as much by the birds of the Hapsburgs as by those of America. There is a considerable variation in size, beginning with those about two inches tall and ranging to specimens more than a foot high and possessing a wing spread of about three feet. The strokes in this carving are bold, the execution that of a man with a keen and sure eye for anatomical details. One of the identifying marks of Schimmel eagles is that of crosshatching, a process in which each feather on wings and body is made to stand out clearly. A usual stance is that in which the bird appears to have alighted, and in a moment more will fold his wings. The base of the block from which this figure has been carved gives no impression of bulkiness, but is nevertheless of sufficient size to hold securely the perfectly proportioned wings and body poised so lightly above it. The wings, incidentally, were made separately and pegged into the body. Traces of brown and black are well defined on most birds, and many of them have had touches of red and black at the eyes and along the strongly curving beak. One of the best preserved specimens of Schimmel's art is an eagle with a maroon body, the feathers picked out in black and white. This resplendent fowl has a white top-knot which appears to make him kin with the so-called bald eagle. The feet and beak are yellow, and the base on which he rests, green. The amount of original paint left on any one of these birds depends largely upon whether it had been kept indoors, as was ordinarily the case with the smaller sizes, or outside, as was the lot of those which tradition says were placed at the top of tall poles near dwelling houses, stores, or even saloons.

Some of the more important pieces are those which appear in groups. Best known among these is the justly celebrated "Garden of Eden," with its figures separately nailed to a board about twenty-four inches by thirty. Occupying the garden, which is enclosed by a picket fence, are a heavily loaded apple tree, the figure of Adam, apple in hand, and Mother Eve, extending still another apple toward her half-reluctant spouse. More accessible to the average collector are the small groupings of birds, now frequently used for mantel ornaments. One good specimen consists of three of these creatures, gaily spotted in red, green, and yellow. The central bird is taller than the other two by virtue of his position atop a cushion pierced by wooden pegs or spikes. (It is thought by some that these apparently meaningless bits of wood were intended to convey the idea of a nest.) Similar groups of two birds, posed either facing or back to back, show equally strong colors. Roosters are sometimes well and smoothly done, but are just as likely to be crude. Likewise to be numbered among the pieces of Schimmel are animals, especially dogs, and lions, tigers, and perhaps others.

A particularly fine type of wood carving, but one come upon very rarely, is the polychrome rooster, resplendent in red comb and wattles, and with a magnificent spread of tail plumes. It was carved from a block about eight inches wide and eight high, the resultant figure giving an impression of rectangularity. The first of the nine tail feathers curves forward almost to the comb, with the rest fanning backward and downward from it. Finer plumage at the rear of the body barely touches the oval-shaped base on which the piece rests, giving it stability without any suggestion of bulkiness. The head, neck, breast, and legs of the bird are gracefully curved. The wings are of a piece with the body, but are outlined in black. The colors, still bright, are red, brown, green, and black on a cream-colored body, with only enough red to give life to the general impression of softly muted cream and brown. Thus far no one has attempted to do much more than guess at the probable place of origin of these birds, no more than a half dozen of which are known. It is a curious fact that while those who own them are all but unanimous in ascribing them to Pennsylvania, they have oftener been found in New York or Connecticut.

More utilitarian but no less attractive among the wood carvings of Pennsylvania are the intaglioed boards known as springerle molds. These devices for decorating flat cakes almost certainly originated in Europe, where they still fulfill their original function. After dough had been rolled to the required degree of thinness, from a quarter to a half inch, it was laid on the mold and firmly pressed so that the details of the design would appear in relief when it was turned over. Those who attempt the operation nowadays may find that applying pressure to the mold laid face down on the dough will give the same result. After the mold had been removed, the cakes were cut apart by a sharp knife before being placed in the oven.

Springerle molds may consist of a simple design, but ordinarily are found as composites of anywhere from six or eight to twenty-four patterns, all carved in exquisite detail. An average specimen consists of eight designs (two wide, four high), the separate units measuring slightly less than two inches each way. A fancy border frames the designs, a different one for each. The various patterns depict a recumbent goat, a summer-house or pergola, a cluster of flowers, a kingfisher, a maiden with a hamper on her back, a cluster of cherries and leaves, and a waterfowl on the wing. The wooden block on the face of which this wealth of detail is lavished is about half an inch thick and of a very fine-grained, heavy wood which has thus far resisted identification, although water-beech, holly, and elm have been suggested. Incising tools of razor-like sharpness have obviously been used, since even the properly serried wing feathers of the water bird are indicated. These designs are by no means the work of an amateur, but of a talented professional who for some reason turned his skill to this lowly task. Not all pieces are so expertly done, but even mediocre ones bear evidences of fine and careful work.

Now and then springerle designs were carved on wooden cylinders which, when fitted with neatly turned handles, became glorified rolling pins. Small rollers with a total of eight patterns have been found, but the more usual type has sixteen designs. One good example contains, along with intricate conventionalized patterns, a carrot, several birds, clusters of fruit, a fish, a Turkish mosque, and a rabbit. In this case some of the designs have been repeated, and the borders are plain. The cylinder itself is made from a heart of quarter-sawed maple.

Neither in the case of the cylinder nor of the flat mold do the details of design give much clue to their probable age. It seems likely that such springerle boards as have survived are from about the middle of the nine-teenth century, but may be a little earlier or later. Unlike some of the Pennsylvania Dutch household implements, they seem to have defied the encroachments of the machine age and have persisted in actual use up to very recent times. It is now possible to buy, in some of the department stores, springerle rolling pins which are a fair approximation of the originals; and for those who would forego the pleasure of actual creation it is possible to buy springerle cakes before Easter in the cities of the Dutchland.

There is an obvious relationship between springerle boards and the in-cised butter molds or markers that have persisted in use up to the present time. Butter molds are of various types, and have been written about so frequently that there is little point in more than mentioning them here. The idea in using them was to beautify pats of butter, both for home consumption and for sale, by stamping or printing a relief design on pounds, half pounds, or even quarter pounds. Occasionally the mold itself was a rectangular trough, with the design at the bottom, and in some instances at the end as well. Molds that cast the butter in hexagonal shape were not unknown. More easily found today are the round molds, fitted with a circular plunger at the end. Butter was packed into the mold with a wooden paddle and then ejected by the plunger, which automatically left the impression of its own intaglio carving in relief on the resultant print. More rarely the plunger bore a design in relief. With hard use and the passing of time the actual molds have often gone to pieces, but the plungers have been preserved, and it is these that are collected today, for the sake of their decorative patterns.

One of the most treasured motifs is that of the cow, which, with well-filled udder, stands peacefully in the shade of a gigantic strawberry blossom. Pasturage is indicated by tufts of grass.   The design of the circular plane within the notched-incised border is well balanced, with cow, flower, foliage, and grass judiciously disposed.   Another attractive mold is a duplicate of a favorite springerle board motif: a pair of conventionalized flowers with enough leaves to give a satisfyingly full effect.   The border is elaborate, consisting of an incised circle followed by a band of carved grooves, these being succeeded by concentric circles up to the actual margin of the wood. Tulips and hearts, of course, are completely representative of German Pennsylvania, and are to be found in a number of variations.   The herringbone-carved tulip is fairly common, and well suited to its purpose.   Another good tulip is the open or full-blown flower also commonly seen on spatterware. The cluster of three feathers seems to be a recurrence of the so-called Prince-of-Wales motif used earlier in fine wood carving and later in pressed glass.

Among specimens well worth adding to one's collection is the eagle, reminiscent of the birds on coins and on all kinds of Federal insignia.   The eagle may face to right or left; he may clutch a sheaf of arrows; he may appear in relief or intaglio, with or without a star or two to give further evidence of his patriotic origin; but always he is a dominant, regal creature.   Other good buys are the sheaf of wheat, which finds a close counterpart in the pattern of a tin cooky cutter, and the acorn, the pine cone, and the pineapple.

A different type of carving ought perhaps, in view of its nature, to be called whittling.   This is the small, hand-cut bracket shelf, the off-the-record product of the boy or man who nowadays would use a jig saw in place of a sharp knife.   Such pieces are not to be confused with the over-ornate Victorian brackets, and corner shelves which at a later date cluttered up so many elegant parlors.   Typical of this work but unique in itself is a wall plaque of pine just under a foot in height.   A single central brace supports a shelf five inches long and three deep.   A cut-out flat heart above the shelf and two quarter circles below it relieve it of an effect of too-great solidity.   The edges of the piece are carved in arabesque patterns well above the shelf, where two red birds perch, one on each side, facing each other.   The sweep of the back is carried up harmoniously to a gently sloping peak, with a diamond-shaped cut-out for hanging it on the wall.   Relieving the brown paint which has been used elsewhere are the red and yellow bodies of the birds, their black top-knots, and three coin-shaped applications of yellow, one above the heart and two below the shelf.   The whole is so smoothly done that it requires a second inspection to reveal the nicety of detail which has gone into the creation of the curved edges.   In fact, the whole thing might be called a study in curves.

Cruder in execution is another wall piece, dated 1802, evidently intended to be hung below a mirror as a receptacle for brush and comb. Nine inches high and seven wide, it has a trough two inches deep in place of a bracket shelf. The back is whittled out in jig-saw fashion, rising to a peak at the top. The two sides approximate each other only roughly. Two different sets of initials appear: A.H.C. on the bottom of the trough, and H.A. on the back. The surface decorations are scratch carved, apparently by a budding geometrician, the result being nine six-pointed "hex" or witch symbols within double circles. Whether by accident or design, one of these remains unfinished. Again, whether to round out the mystical number nine, or for some less obscure reason, the maker, having exhausted the available space on the back and on the outer surfaces, put the ninth circle on an inside end of the trough. Double lines in freehand, following the curves of the back, help to give a finished appearance to this little oddity. A similar comb case, but of much finer workmanship, is known to have been the work of George Huguenin, of Newfoundland, Pennsylvania. Huguenin's work will be discussed later in connection with toy carving.

Related to these pieces in form and design are the extremely scarce, carved wall spoon racks of a very early day. These were larger pieces, crudely executed, with narrow, notched shelves into which spoons could be hung by the bowl. Some were severely rectangular; others had shaped or molded edges and were decorated with scratch carving. A good specimen, now in the possession of the Metropolitan Museum, is about eighteen inches long and nine wide and has three shelves, each of which is intended to accommodate four spoons. Designs of "hex" marks enclosed in circles appear on the entire surface. The basic color is a dark blue, the incised patterns being picked out in red, white, green, and yellow. A less ornate specimen, but with the hex-markings in evidence, was offered for sale at an antique show very recently.

Similar in feeling is a linen presser dated 1799. The presser is a flat board about twenty inches long and six wide, with a knob at one end and a handle shaped like that of a mason's trowel at the other. Painted in brown, this unique piece bears a central decoration of a red tulip, with buds springing from each side of its long stem. Unfortunately for the average collector, such examples of Pennsylvania Dutch artistry are seldom or never to be come upon except in museums.

A fairly late manifestation of wood carving is to be found in open dressers and on heavy chairs and spring rockers, here and there in rural areas. These patterns are of the utmost simplicity, consisting merely of gouged-out shallows to indicate conventionalized leaf and flower forms. In itself this carving would hardly merit attention, though perhaps in time, as finer pieces grow more and more scarce, it will find its devotees.

In addition to the carved articles listed in the foregoing pages, the diligent searcher will now and then come across still others, usually of a more humble nature.   Wooden bake boards were sometimes enhanced by having a heart-shaped cut-out instead of an ordinary nail hole for use when it was to be hung away.   Cabbage cutters were similarly treated, as were the handles of tubs.   Cradles frequently showed an attempt at this kind of beautification, as did the low shoe polishing bench.   If by chance the reader is a collector of heart-decorated wooden ware, he may find in Dutch Pennsylvania a good many hitherto undiscovered treasures of this sort.

Kitchen Stuff

As anyone who has pursued a study of the domestic affairs of the Pennsylvania Germans will realize instantly, the kitchen was the most important room in the house. It goes almost without saying that the appurtenances to cookery are varied, ingenious, and worthy of a detailed consideration beyond what can be given here. For the householder who has the means to re-create a Pennsylvania kitchen in his own establishment, a faithful study of the collections in the historical museums, rather than a book, is to be recommended. Only in that way can the infinitely varied cookery implements, the vessels of iron, copper, and brass, and the products of the cooper's trade be understood and appreciated. On the other hand, the average collector who has fallen in love with a bright copper ladle, a lap coffee grinder, or an iron muffin pan need not stifle all his acquisitive instincts just because it is out of the question for him to set up a small museum of his own. For him it is merely a question of using good taste in acquiring articles which he can actually use, or display to good advantage in an unpretentious setting. Out of a myriad of objects once found in spring house, storage room, cellar kitchen, and summer kitchen such will be mentioned here as seem to offer possibilities for successful transplantation.

The fireplace comes to mind first of all, and here andirons were a necessity, as were the pokers and tongs needed to keep the burning logs in order. While the actual tools of the hearth were generally of the utmost simplicity, the andirons often showed signs of imaginative craftsmanship. Slender upright posts of wrought iron terminated in spheres, cones, or cubes, or in tapering ends bent back in the form of a circle. In later times cast iron brought in vase-shaped and globe-topped forms. The American Revolution put the Hessian soldier into many a fireplace, and since he was practically indestructible he is still found now and then. Both the Hessian and the owl, which presumably came later, have been reproduced. Ships, houses, and others of doubtful Pennsylvania provenance have been listed, as well as many nondescript patterns more useful than beautiful. The finer brass articles so sought after today are hard to distinguish from those to be found elsewhere in the land.

A number of years ago there was considerable interest in the ornate stove plates of cast iron which formed the sides of the box-like successor to the open fireplace.   Heavy and cumbersome, they offer little allure to the general collector, but they are completely representative of the Dutchland, with their wide range of Biblical scenes and quotations and their intricate designs, among which the tulip was a prime favorite.   Perhaps most of the really fine specimens are now in the Bucks County Historical Museum at Doylestown, Pennsylvania.

Naturally the great open fireplace and its attendant bake oven called for specialized implements.   First there were the iron cooking pots of all sizes, which hung from the crane itself or from trammels which could be adjusted to regulate the distance of the pot from the coals.   Large cast-iron kettles with a capacity of many gallons were once used for heating water, for rendering lard, for making soap, and for other large-scale operations. Smaller iron pots were used for all the ordinary stewing and boiling, and flat-bottomed Dutch ovens which stood on stubby legs directly over the coals took care of minor baking operations.   More to the taste of the present-day housekeeper, who might find it difficult to utilize a cast-iron pot, are the vessels of shining brass or softly glowing copper.   A row of copper sauce pans of graduated sizes, a long-handled copper ladle, a basin, a goose-neck teakettle, a copper Turk's-head mold tin-plated on the inside—these would lend distinction to any fireplace striving for an old-time air.   One collector has secured enough fine copper pieces to take care of all her kitchen needs. Expensive but probably worth all they cost are the copper kettles with heavy bails, only a little larger in diameter at the top than at the bottom.   They are extremely light in weight, even mammoth apple-butter cauldrons more than two feet high weighing but a few pounds.   Since the original purchase price of these vessels was rather high, it was not uncommon for families to own them in partnership, trading them back and forth in the fall at apple-butter time.   Woe to the luckless youth who let his cornhusk-tipped paddle pause even for an instant in the day-long stirring chore, for in a few seconds a burn would develop which it would take hours of patient scrubbing to remove from the thin metal!

The brass buckets and utensils of the Pennsylvania Dutch household lend themselves to a variety of uses not confined to the kitchen.   The buckets themselves can be used for fruit, flowers, or house plants, for kindling wood, or for any of a dozen everyday purposes.   Tall brass coffee pots which may have served at church dinners or gatherings of the *Freundsschaft* (friends and relatives) may fill a special need for some collectors.   And, of course, there are brass candlesticks, brass lamps, brass ladles and skimmers, brass coggling wheels for pastry, and brass teakettles—to say nothing of long-handled brass warming pans which have long outlived their original function of removing the chill from icy sheets.

Of particular interest because of their attractive designs are the long-handled waffle irons, which were heated in the fireplace, filled with batter, and then laid back on the coals. The heart and the tulip, as might be expected, were often to be found, and are most popular with collectors. Anyone who has braved the heat of open-hearth cookery will be able to appreciate the long handles of these implements, as of most of the cooking tools used. The elongated wrought-iron shanks of skimmers frequently terminated in tulip-shaped, heart-shaped, or rat-tailed finials, as did flat turners, immense iron spoons, two-tined forks, and ladles of all sizes.

Trivets placed over the embers accommodated iron skillets small and large, as well as flat-bottomed cooking pots and iron tea kettles. These three-legged contrivances were often gracefully shaped and finely patterned, and merit the attention of the seeker after the unusual. Toasters were ingeniously fashioned in designs as airy as any lavished on the tall candle stands of New England. Some were intended to stand vertically, convenient iron guards at the base holding the slices of bread more or less firmly in place. Others rested horizontally on the hearth, the bread standing erect between the bars of a semi-circular framework. A swivel arrangement in this type of toaster gave it the name of "self-turning." The bread toasters and waffle irons seem to have been peculiar to Pennsylvania, but the various long spoons, forks, and skimmers are such as were patterned at most of the home forges of Colonial times. In a shop, an unidentified long spoon or fork might have come from New England or the South, but if the slender rod of iron has been flattened at the end and wrought into the form of a tulip or a heart it is a safe guess that a beauty-loving Pennsylvania Dutchman was its maker.

Flat silverware of the Pennsylvania Germans seems to have been no different from that of other families able to afford such a comparative luxury, just as the early pewter seems to have differed but little from its New England or Southern counterpart. Vastly more research than has yet been done will be needed before a peculiarly Pennsylvania Dutch preference in either silver or pewter can be demonstrated in a convincing manner.

Characteristic of Pennsylvania, though, are the "Welsh Mountain" horn-handled knives and forks of good English steel. The knives are broad-bladed and flexible, with round ends and slightly curving backs. The handles are made from sections of deer's antlers, held firmly in place by tiny steel pins. The ends are plugged with wood to which a rounded metal cap is fastened by means of two more pins. Each cap has been shaped to fit its individual handle, whether large or small, round or oval. A "set" of knives or of forks is a set in name only, for each handle differs from its neighbors in shape, color, texture, and degree of curvature. Forks are two-tined and average about two inches shorter than the usual ten of the knives. The knives apparently were made to bear the brunt of eating, since the forks were obviously intended only to anchor large portions of meat or other food, and horn-handled spoons are missing entirely.

Most of the knives carry the impressed names of their manufacturers. Among these appear "Wm. Jackson & Co., Sheaf Island Works, Sheffield," "W. Greaves & Sons, Cast Steel," and "Wilson Hawes Worth & Moss," this last with a crown above it between the initials VR, presumably for Victoria Regina. The forks are unmarked. The term "Welsh Mountain" has been applied to these knives and forks because they were first observed in that part of the Dutch country, not because they were made there, as had been claimed before the stamped impressions of English names removed any last shadow of doubt.

Later knives and forks, far enough removed from contemporary patterns to be considered collectible, include plain white, bone-handled ones inset with metal ferrules in various patterns. The forks of these are three-tined. Knives and forks in any of these categories are becoming increasingly hard to find, principally because collectors who have a wide range among china and glass for table settings have discovered a paucity of cutlery. Pewter spoons can be pressed into service, especially those with a tulip design. Lacking these, the housewife will probably have to eke out her service with silver of non-Pennsylvania Dutch provenance or eat as did the early farmers!

For the accommodation of the short-handled tableware, wooden knife boxes were commonly employed. Ordinarily these were severely plain, having two compartments separated by a central partition with a heart-shaped or other cut-out at the top serving in place of a handle. The sides and ends of the box sloped outward for convenience.

A unique specimen among knife boxes came to light a few years back when a collector, impressed by the fact that a particularly dingy object, heavily encrusted with paint, had hinged covers for the knife and fork sections, added it rather dubiously to her other purchases. Successive applications of varnish remover revealed a fine walnut box inlaid with designs in cherry, mahogany, holly, maple, fruit wood, and ebony on every outer surface. One lid bears a knife mosaic, above and around which are grouped the figures of a man, a horse, a clover leaf, and five inch-long diamond-shaped inlays of holly. The opposite lid has a fork as the central motif, with clover leaves and conventional patterns accompanying it. The handle contains the inset initials "A.A.E." Figures of barnyard animals, various leaves, and five-pointed stars pretty well fill the space between edgings of woods set in contrasting colors. As a final touch the lids and the upper edge of the handle are studded with tiny insets of holly. All in all it is a remarkable specimen of handwork, and one which cost its maker many an hour of patient labor.

Some knife boxes are large enough to use as carrying trays, and offer an especially convenient way of handling glasses. Pine is most often used, with walnut a close second. Now and then an early nail box of the kind used by carpenters is found in so fine a condition that it is promoted to the pantry, or given the job of holding small pots of flowers.

The difficulty of obtaining hollow utensils in early times, especially before tin replaced many of the heavy iron pots and pans, forced our ancestors to resort to many makeshift devices. Among small, light utensils were those made from gourds, which grew (and can still be grown by those who have a sunny garden) in great profusion. Dipper gourds of considerable antiquity, considering their perishable nature, linger on in modern times, although not in actual service. Gourds served for bottles, for cups and bowls, for darning eggs, and for nest eggs. The pithy contents of one variety, when properly treated and dried, even made an acceptable substitute for a dish cloth.

Gourd baskets, elaborately painted in red, black, yellow, and brown, were made to serve a decorative purpose. A typical specimen is elliptical-shaped, its shorter diameter being about seven inches and the longer one nine. The inch-wide handle has been formed by cutting away what amounts to quarter sections on each side of the upper half of the fruit. The rim of the basket itself has been fancifully scalloped. Before painting, the artisan smoothed out the interior so that only a shell remained, and now, after years of slow desiccation, it is of paper thinness. With its bright colors and pleasing proportions, this basket is but one more evidence of the urge toward beauty that motivated the so-called "stolid" Pennsylvania Dutchmen.

Still other Dutch-country finds, sometimes attractive, sometimes merely curious, might be mentioned. For instance, there is the pair of wrought-iron extension tongs used by the pipe-smoker to extract a live coal from the open hearth. This gadget is a spiritual companion to the early folding extension candle holder. The iron apple-peeler and corer was most useful at apple-butter time. Pie crust crimpers are sometimes commonplace, sometimes unique; a wrought-iron specimen with a fanciful bird finial would certainly fall in the latter category. Heavy iron door stops in the shape of frogs or beetles are notable. Coffee mills, not especially early, are snapped up as fast as they come to market. And so it goes. The serious collector, especially one who has access to shops out of the beaten path, may find half a hundred items from exquisite Kentucky ("Kentucky" in name only, since they were largely made in Pennsylvania) rifles to fish-shaped weather vanes or calico block-print molds, all attesting to the talent so long overlooked in the Dutchland.

Miniatures and Toys

"You can't have that," says the antiques dealer; "I'm saving it for my little daughter." That is the story more than one collector has heard in the Dutchland, and while he will immediately experience the sense of frustration which seems to strike hardest at the hunter balked of his prey, he will also be forced to concede the appropriateness of the reservation. Some of the most appealing mementos of the old days are those objects which, created for children, belong to them forever. Whether or not it is ethical for the dealer to exhibit something he has no intention of selling is another matter, and one that is, perhaps, beside the point.

More than a few of the artisans responsible for the furniture and house-keeping equipment of rural homes turned their hands to miniatures or play-things either for their own children or for those of customers. This seems to have been especially true of cabinetmakers, for play furniture is a fairly common survival. Possibly the most attractive pieces are the painted-decorated ones which approximate their larger prototypes in design and coloring—in everything, in fact, except size. A necessary distinction must be made between the articles actually intended for children's use, and those which were presumably for their dolls. Doll-house gear, or what might be called true miniatures, lacks the sturdiness of construction that is demanded by actual usage.

Chairs, painted in cream, green, yellow, or brown to match those needed by the adults of the household are well worth securing, whether there are children in the family or not. The floral patterns used in the decorations are essentially the same as those mentioned in an earlier chapter on the subject, although occasionally abbreviated because of the smaller expanse of surface in which the artist had to work. The seat of the chair, the central splat of the back, the top rail, all bore the floral, fruit, or bird patterns used in furniture of the regular size. Red as a basic color, while not often used elsewhere, was apparently considered suitable for small furniture. Chairs with rockers were often preferred to the straight variety, and display superior decorations. The bowback Windsor was a popular pattern, in Pennsylvania as elsewhere.

Two well-done settees, duplicates in little of the characteristic Dutch bench, have been noted recently. The first is about twenty-four inches long, with the seat about ten inches from the floor. The details of legs, seat, and back are of only average workmanship, but the floral decorations, creamy pink roses and green leaves on a dark brown ground, are excellent. The piece shows evidence of use, but is very sturdy. The second bench, perhaps twenty-eight inches in length, is painted a bright red, the ornamentation being principally in gilt stenciling. As a deterrent to enamored collectors, the dealer placed a price on them more than commensurate with those of the full-sized article. For all that, they were soon sold.

Small chests of drawers were faithful reproductions of what was currently fashionable. One of these in the early Empire feeling, made by a coffin- and cabinetmaker for his nine-year-old daughter, is a masterpiece of construction. Measuring fourteen inches high, fifteen long and ten deep, it has three long drawers below and two shorter ones above. The wood is cherry. The swelling bow front and the drawers are veneered in expertly matched crotch mahogany. Once upon a time it no doubt served to house the wardrobe of a family of dolls, but now, as a repository for needles, pins, and spools of thread, it occupies a place of honor atop a low chest of drawers in the cherry-furnished bedroom of the little girl's grown-up grand-daughter.

A painted chest of similar proportions but without the swell front made its appearance at several consecutive antique shows a few years ago. With its pink roses festooned against a cream-painted background, it presented a charming appearance. At least one visitor waited hopefully for the last night of the show, hoping that the owner might shade the steep price a little rather than carry the chest home again. When the expected bargain failed to materialize, the visitor discovered that the dealer had been raising the price two dollars after each show, hoping in that way eventually to compensate herself for transporting it back and forth. No doubt by now the little bureau has become priceless.

The usual accompaniment of the doll's bureau was the cradle of walnut, cherry, or pine, the exact counterpart of the larger ones now being used for newspapers, periodicals, or even for kindling wood. One of these tiny beds on rockers enjoys the distinction of having cradled the daughter of its present owner when that unexpectedly-diminutive young woman made her appearance in the world, truly a notable feat for a bit of furniture twelve inches long. Still other miniature pieces include beds, kitchen cupboards, and bucket benches.

If one wishes to do so, he may occasionally be able to buy Dutch dolls at the same time he buys the furniture. There are dealers who specialize in this field, and who make a point of authentic costumes. Occasionally even the doll's name and ancestry are supplied as part of the transaction. There are rag dolls stuffed with sawdust, jointed wooden dolls, and dolls with papier mâché, bisque, or china heads. In most cases it must be admitted that there is nothing especially Dutch about them, in the sense of characteristics that do not appear elsewhere in the country. Dolls of good quality were practically always distributed through city stores, with no reference to a particular destination. For those who wish dolls dressed in the authentic clothing of the Pennsylvania Dutch sectarians there are excellent specimens on the market. Bonneted Mennonites in gray, Amish girls in bright colors, and Amish boys in broad-brimmed hats are to be found in gift shops and at road-side stands in the Dutch country. They have been made with care and are dressed in the actual colors and materials used by the sectarians.

Within the last few years statuettes and figurines in authentic garb have been offered for sale. Some are in excellently carved wood, others in cast iron. Mennonites, Amish, and the River Brethren are in this list. The cast-iron figures make interesting paper weights. Some have real merit as art objects. The customary size range is from two to seven inches. A typical pair is the Amish man and his wife. The man has black trousers and vest, a blue shirt, and a broad, black hat. His red hair is worn long, and he has a fringe of red beard. His wife wears a blue dress, a black apron, and a black bonnet. She has a touch of white at her throat, and like her husband has red hair. This color is authentic, since one subdivision of the Amish is composed almost entirely of red-heads.

Appealing to children and adults alike are the bellows toys which used to make their appearance under the Christmas tree, but which are far too valuable today to risk in so vulnerable a spot. These toys were of papier mâché painted in naturalistic colors. Birds and barnyard fowl were oftenest represented, with the robin and the rooster as prime favorites. In place of legs, thin twisted spirals of stout wire attached the body of the bird to the rectangular bellows base. The base itself consisted of thin strips of wood at top and bottom, the sides being formed of strips of muslin or canvas. A small spring inside, and a whistle at the base completed the toy, which was operated by depressing the raised end of the bellows. The spring brought the bellows back to its original position, the motion causing the bird to teeter on his wire legs at the same time that the whistle gave him a voice. The purchaser will probably have to be satisfied with a bird in only reasonably good condition, as the papier mâché did not provide too satisfactory a foundation for the heavy coatings of paint. The colors vary in hue, but red, yellow, green, and brown are common. A typical rooster stands five inches in height and possesses red comb, eyes, wattles, and wing sheaths. The body color is a pinkish buff, while the tail plumes are green, red, yellow, and black. The feet are painted, in black, on the upper surface of the bellows.

Other Christmas tree ornaments, or ornaments intended for the *putz*, the decorative landscape which accompanied the tree, also persist into modern

BURL CHERRY CHEST

WALNUT CHEST: BRIDE'S BOX

times. Some of the towns and cities and many of the rural areas in the
Dutchland carry on the tradition of Christmas *putzen* as heartily as they did
a hundred years and more ago, often using the original figures of the crèche
and of the entire Nativity scene as long as they will hold together. Among
those which at rare intervals find their way to the antique shop are the wood
carvings which trace their ancestry straight to Switzerland and to Germanic
toy-carving areas. It is all but impossible to distinguish an American-made
toy sheep, for instance, from its European counterpart, and unless there is
a direct line of ancestry back to the carver the idea of authenticating might
as well be given up.

One George Huguenin, descendant of a French-Swiss family of Travere,
came to this country about the middle of the nineteenth century, bringing
with him the inherited skill of the wood carvers of his native Switzerland.
His procedure, as described by his descendants, was first of all to build and
carve a stable according to a Swiss original. Next he would fashion the
creatures of the barnyard—sheep, cattle, horses, hens, roosters and so on,
but with the principal emphasis on sheep. It has even been suggested that
the barn itself and the rest of the barnyard occupants were made to serve
merely as a plausible background for these favorite animals. The Huguenin
sheep were not carved of one piece of wood but of several, the legs and tail
being executed separately and then joined to the rest of the animal. The
same method was followed by other carvers who specialized in Noah's Ark
animals. These were smaller by half than Huguenin's figures, often measuring less than an inch in height. Such exotic creatures as lions, elephants,
giraffes, zebras and, in fact, all the denizens of the zoo were meticulously
whittled out of wood and then painted. Among them all, only Huguenin's
sheep appear to have been equipped with an honest-to-goodness pelt, for
whereas other carvers depended upon a coat of paint for the final touch, he
used actual wool. For some reason one of his black sheep was in existence
long after its white-coated companions had lived out their allotted span of
years.

Other Huguenin carvings included tiny farmhouses, each formed out of
a single block of wood, except for the chimney. These dwellings were not
more than two inches high. Doors and windows were outlined in black
against a white background. None of his circus figures appear to be in
existence, although his daughter remembers horses specially constructed to
carry miniature china clowns with wired arms and legs.

In the main, circus, Noah's Ark or other similar toy carvings that can
be bought commercially show varying degrees of desirability. Some are
very late, and under their glistening paint show definite traces of machine
carving. Still, because of a steadily growing demand for miniatures, they

have usually found a market, with genuinely old ones that even a mere decade or two ago would hardly have been thought worth bothering with.

Another item of early Christmas tree garniture is the blown glass ornament, most often in the form of a bunch of grapes. Gaily colored in green, amethyst, silver, and various rainbow tones, these rather heavy affairs, said to have been made in South Jersey, show to good advantage when hung in a window, or when piled in a burl bowl for use as a centerpiece. Candlesticks with tiny fluted cups and long, bent wires looped over a branch of the tree and culminating in heavy "bobs" at the bottom once menaced with their lighted candles the entire collection of paper and tinsel ornaments, papier mâché birds, and all the myriads of objects which comprised the Christmas tree decorations. The inevitable passing of these homespun articles is to be lamented, for with them have gone, all but unrecorded, some of the most interesting products of folk ingenuity. The filigree baskets of silver-like metal filled with marzipan, the puzzling interlocked circlets carved out of a single piece of wood, the jointed acrobatic wooden dolls, the blown glass bubbles on strings: these and others have largely perished, or at least rarely come to the attention of the collector.

Play dishes, that is, chinaware or pottery in miniature, have fared better. Miniatures in spatterware, while not common, are found often enough to make the search worth while. Handleless cups in plain green, yellow, red, and blue, with or without saucers, as well as later handled cups serve as specimens of Dutchiana for those with a minimum of display space. Tea sets consisting of tea pot, sugar bowl, and creamer have been offered in the hard-to-find green spatter, and in the peafowl design at that. Butter chips and cup plates, which are of course not true miniatures, go very well with other small-scale pieces. A fairly late plain blue set of sixty pieces, including plates, cups, saucers and indeed all the items that could be used in setting a tea table, came on the market a year or so ago. Admittedly this plain blue is less desirable than the patterned forms.

Another of the typically Dutch tablewares to be found in miniature is the Gaudy Welsh. Tea sets of this richly colored china are merely replicas of the larger pieces mentioned previously. No Gaudy Dutch miniatures seem to have been reported.

Kitchen equipment, perhaps only in later years, often numbered small utensils for the youngsters who were at the age when they wished to "help" their mothers. Miniature cooky cutters, pie dishes, fluted cake tins, and the like are not uncommon. One dealer has a very extensive collection of such items, some of them merely playthings, others such as saw actual use. Among them all, none are more attractive than the flat, heart-shaped Moravian mint-candy tins which, in addition to their regular function, served as molds for maple sugar and for small cakes.

Now and then in an obscure corner of a country shop a coin bank comes to light—not the mechanical bank of popular fancy, though that type was also known to the Dutch country, but the molded pottery bank with a cut-out slot in the top, sometimes large enough to receive a silver dollar. These banks are generally of red or yellow glazed earthenware, the workmanship often not conspicuously good. Hens and ducks were especially popular.

Peculiar to the Dutch country, apparently, was the custom of "engraving" Easter eggs. Of course, so colorful a custom as dyeing eggs by means of onion skins or commercial vegetable dyes was heartily endorsed, but hours were spent in many homes on scratch-carving all manner of patterns on the surface of a single egg, usually one intended as a gift. That such presents were treasured is obvious from the number that have remained intact. Names of the giver and the recipient, the date, representations of trees, birds, and animals, to say nothing of fancy borders and arabesques—all these were incised lightly on the shell of the dyed egg.

An appealing story is told about an unusual Easter egg decorated long ago in the Dutchland. It was the custom in a certain school to give the teacher a present at Easter, with colored eggs the favorite gift. One poor youngster had no color for such a purpose, and no money to buy the necessary dye. In desperation, as she wandered about, wrestling with her problem, she gathered some chips lying near the chopping block. She knew the virtues of butternut and of hemlock bark in dyeing wool, and hoped that by some miracle she might produce a red or green which would be the envy of her classmates. Carefully she prepared the brew and put the egg in to color—but when it came out it was black. She had only one egg she might use for the purpose; so to avoid the anticipated jeers of her companions she proceeded to scratch through the black surface to the white underneath, in an attempt to do something that no one else had done. Close to the larger end of the egg she made a base line, and upon it drew a beehive. Next to the beehive appeared a tree, with each leaf distinctly outlined. Beyond the tree she placed a currant bush, and between that and the starting point two large roses springing straight from the earth on tall stems. The teacher was pleased by the gift, so pleased that she kept it ever after. That was a long time ago; just how long, we know because the young artist took such pride in her achievement that she supplied a record beneath the beehive: "Sally Groff, March 30th, 1864."

Not too many eggs, of course, have survived, but they are still to be found. Egg "pitchers" are more rare. These playthings were made by encasing the egg in a strip of calico just wide enough to make a base so that the egg would stand on end. A handle for the pitcher was created by means of a loop of the same fabric. Empty egg shells were often dyed at Easter time, and no doubt one of these shells, furbished up by the bit of bright cotton, made a very satisfying addition to the dolls' tea table. Eggs intended for this purpose were pierced at each end with a darning needle, and the contents blown into a mixing bowl, after which the ends were closed with a bit of paraffin or candle wax.

As a final suggestion for re-creation of a section of the past through the use of small things rather than large, one might recommend the scrapbooks which were popular a mere fifty years ago. Until only yesterday these great volumes gathered dust along with other Victorian and post-Victorian relics too ugly for use but too good to throw away. Eventually, of course, they were remembered and their brilliant contents re-appraised. It is only an occasional scrapbook that is worth much in itself, since most of the bindings have gone to pieces, and the pages are often stained and torn. However, the highly embossed and brilliantly colored pictures used as paste-ins are not only innately attractive but lend themselves to a variety of modern uses. A large department store features boxes to which they have been pasted, and covered with a protecting coat of shellac. Occasional whole pages are lifted from scrapbooks and framed. Under the glass top of a coffee table or a tray they sparkle as brilliantly as they did in the day when they were traded back and forth as a common currency of childhood. They have been grouped to good effect on lamp shades.

These bits of paper are almost a product of the machine age, since they were turned out in mass quantities after lithographing and color processing had become commonplace. They may be grouped most conveniently according to their intended uses. First there are the smaller cut-outs which were primarily for pasting into books. These include a tremendous variety of roses, violets, and other flowers; exotic birds with brilliant plumage; animals from the aardvark to the zebra; glossy reptiles and feartul dragons; characters in ornate costume from the ends of the earth—Russia, China, India; and certainly not the least noteworthy, an infinite variety of cherubs' faces, smiling, pouting, sleeping, and screaming.

A second group is the type used for greeting card decoration. Elaborate sprays of roses, violets, forget-me-nots, and lilies-of-the-valley served as a background for clasped hands, or a hand-and-heart composition. So that there might be no mistake, the words "Forever Thine," "Faithful to the End" or others often appeared on a ribbon among the flowers. The embossed flower cut-out was pasted at one end to a deckle-edged fringed name card, the name itself being concealed by the flowers.

Christmas motifs form almost a complete group in themselves, with a size range of from a quarter inch in height to about three inches. Santa Claus heads are no less colorful than full-length figures with overflowing packs. Lighted Christmas trees vie in interest with wreaths and clusters of holly and mistletoe. Very late, but collectors' items for all that, are the first automobiles, with St. Nick at the wheel and the tonneau bulging with gifts. After the scrapbook fad had run its course these figures were carried over into contemporary times as Christmas seals.

Of more historical interest than the preceding groups are the Christmas and New Year's cards of the eighties and the nineties, which were printed in colors but not embossed. They are usually dated, and mirror faithfully the costumes of the times. Some of them, as a matter of fact, served as advertisements for clothing stores. Seasonal cards of this sort usually measured about three by five inches or slightly larger. Attractive because of their composition and color, they are also excellent genre pictures of their day.

The buyer who picks up his first scrap book is cautioned to look through it rather well before buying. Scrapbooks contain many things besides greeting cards and gilded and embossed bits of ornamentation. Children frequently ran out of material before their pages were filled, and resorted to the seed catalogues. Flowers and vegetables of surpassing beauty and size were shown in full color in those days as well as now—and were painstakingly transferred to the scrapbook. In fact, colored representations of all sorts, not even excepting wall paper, fraternized comfortably there with their elders and betters.

Interesting as they are to the present generation of collectors of Pennsylvania Dutchiana, these paste-ins and cards are not peculiarly Pennsylvanian; in many cases they were actually imported from Germany, and were widely distributed over the entire country. Their bright colors and attractive forms made them especially welcome in Pennsylvania, however; at least if the number surviving in scrapbooks may be counted as evidence.

Ornamental Objects

So fond were the Pennsylvania Dutch of gay colors and design, both in things of their own creating and in what they bought, that any attempt to draw a line between what was purely ornamental and what had originally been intended as utilitarian must be an arbitrary one. The Dutch have always been notable for withholding the finest of their possessions from active use, and for substituting a second best or even a third best within the bosom of the family. Had it not been for that happy state of affairs, today's collector would fare less well than he does. Perhaps the Schimmel carvings should be listed as non-utilitarian, although certainly some of them served as toys in the old days. In any event, even the purely ornamental objects were produced because of a need for relief from the monotony of everyday life and surroundings, and must be given something of a utilitarian status on that account.

Included in this class of rural art objects are the "chalk" ornaments, actually plaster of Paris, which have become steadily scarcer in recent years as collectors have come to show an interest in them. It seems likely that these figures, intended as mantel garnitures, found their inspiration in the not dissimilar Staffordshire pottery, perhaps because, while the Staffordshire ware was not actually expensive, plaster of Paris was considerably cheaper.

Some of the available chalk may date back to the year 1768, when Henry Christian Geyer of Boston advertised "Plaister of Paris" parrots, dogs, lions, and other items, but in the Dutch country no such venerable antiquity has as yet been established. It is within the realm of possibility, of course, but it is a known fact that peddlers were selling trayfuls of plaster parrots, canaries, vases, and "cathedral pieces" from door to door in the 1850's and that, in fact, identical ornaments were being dispersed in the Dutchland almost to the end of the century. The problem of establishing the exact age of a specimen therefore becomes an extremely complicated one and one that the experts, probably wisely, have not tried too hard to solve. The wonder is that so much chalk has remained intact, since it is light in weight, often top-heavy, and extremely fragile.

Chalk pieces were usually cast in two-part molds, the separate halves then being joined before decoration took place. Thus most genuine pieces

134

are hollow, although now and then the bases were partly or completely filled with a cheap clay for added stability.   Novices are sometimes advised that hollowness in chalkware is a sure sign of genuineness, but the statement is not entirely true.   The inevitable counterfeiters (most of whom are well known to bona fide dealers) have been able to duplicate everything but the actual colors of chalk.   Their difficulty in surmounting the final hurdle lies in the curious fact that age brings about a change in the texture of the surface to which color has been applied, and as yet no artificial aging method has been discovered.

The forms of chalkware oftenest found are those of birds, animals, and fruit.   Among the animal forms dogs, cats, lions, and deer were prime favorites, with squirrels and sheep following.   French poodles, properly clipped, are commonly shown on their haunches.   An unusually fine one has been found in cream, with ears, eyes, and coat-bandings in black, collar and mouth in red.   This dog is just under five inches in height.   Other beasts of more or less indeterminate breed are shown in similar positions, as well as in erect and recumbent poses.   Eyes, eyebrows, and facial markings are very prominent, sometimes with ludicrous effect.

Cats are often quite large, occasionally life size, and are shown in various naturalistic attitudes.   As in the case of dogs, the color was applied with a brush, frequently in happy-go-lucky fashion.   Cats' whiskers are usually very prominent, but not very convincing, since they often suggest the lines of a mask.   Deer are almost always shown reclining, and rather closely resemble those of Bennington pottery in form.   Because of their rarity they have frequently been reproduced.   The new tan and buff colorings are usually a give-away, since they are both too light and too clean.   The squirrels of chalkware habitually carry nuts in their forepaws.   Sheep are recumbent, and bear less resemblance than dogs to their Staffordshire prototypes.

Birds include both domestic and wild fowls, all of which have their wings folded.   Roosters, hens, parrots, eagles, and others bear a close resemblance not only to the wooden birds of Schimmel but to the native redware pottery forms which will be mentioned later.

Fruit pieces of chalk in good condition are considerably harder to secure than animals and birds, but are by no means non-existent.   A year or two ago a suburban lady, making a hurried exit from the antique department of a large city store, discovered a good specimen which had been used as a lamp base.   She turned over the price tag, mentally cataloguing her afternoon's purchases and wondering whether she had money enough for this piece, which even in its mutilated condition had at once become a "must." The price was so low that it was obvious that whoever had priced it did not know its real value.   Patiently she waited through the interminable time of checking and wrapping, for so important a piece must be carried by hand

and not trusted to the mercies of a package delivery. Finally she boarded her train, two hours after the time she had told her husband to meet her. On the way from the station she almost blurted out the secret but refrained, thinking of the triumphal moment of unwrapping. When she got out of the car at home she handed the package to her husband, remarking as she did so, "Handle this carefully; it's fragile." He placed it on the top of several other packages and turned to follow her up the steps to the house. But he slipped on the bottom one and fell, landing with his full weight directly on the treasured chalkware. Not even a piece as large as a half dollar remained intact. Perhaps at some remotely distant date the incident may come to have its lighter side, but so far it still has all the elements of tragedy.

The fruit pieces were also cast in two molds. Only the front section was colored. The apple-like fruits were painted in tones of green, red, and yellow, with occasional markings in black. The apples, if apples they be, were pyramided sharply, with leaves at the top and between the separate fruits. These pieces are shallower than somewhat similar but bowl-like representations. Occasionally single oranges were made, with green leaves creating a pyramidal frame for them, and, rarely, shapes suggesting a pineapple but in a bright blue.

Less common are human figures; ornate pseudo-Gothic cathedral fronts with spaces ("windows") for candles; and plaster watch cases, pillared half-domes with an opening behind which a pocket watch could be slipped. Watch cases are crudely done, the classic effect of the columns being obscured by indiscriminate streakings of bright color. Plaster-of-Paris houses and family groups may or may not be of Pennsylvania provenance, but are similar in feeling and merit the consideration of the collector.

Somewhat akin to ornamental fruit chalk is a type of native majolica which represented bowls or plates filled with vegetables realistically colored. Some of this ware, perhaps all of it, was made at Phoenixville in Pennsylvania, and was widely distributed. Plates of peas, lima beans or asparagus, and bowls of cauliflower are known. Sugar bowls and creamers designed to look like cabbages were favorites, as were pitchers in the general shape of ears of corn. In every case the colorings were remarkably faithful to the models. Such pieces do not mix well with other tableware, but in a place of their own may be rather attractive.

Also deserving of a place of their own are the purely ornamental shelf figures turned out by the early potters in their offhand moments. Of native clay, they were glazed and burned at the same time and in the same way as the more utilitarian bowls, jugs, and pie plates. Some were probably intended for playthings; most of them found then, as they do today, an honored place on the mantel.

Unique in form is the fan-shaped pottery flower vase, the holders of which project upward from the ring-shaped water vessel somewhat like the fingers of a glove. The amateur is hardly likely to come upon one of these, although a rare specimen is found now and then. Ornamental birds, not too finely detailed, and occasional animals, usually dogs, are easier to get. Fine glazing characterizes some of these pieces, and mottlings of green and brownish purple are sometimes noted. The poodle, either plain or in the form of a penny bank with a slotted back, is a good choice. Better still is the green-purple-brown Saint Bernard with his little brandy cask. Bird banks are commoner than dog banks. Often the capacity of these receptacles is so limited that it would appear that they were intended for show rather than for use. More capacious were the book-banks of brown mottled pottery, and the unique Empire bureau-bank which brought a record price at a New York auction a few years back.

Now and then lavishly ornamented sugar bowls, "baskets," and tobacco jars were fired by the potters, as well as flower pots and jardinieres with incised ornamentation and coggled borders, but so rarely that a description of them would be a mere repetition of what museum publications have to say about them. Bennington-like candlesticks are worth a round sum, and are actually more attractive to many without than with candles. Fancy jugs with spigots, covered butter dishes, and fish dishes add to the list. Glazed ornamental tiles are come upon now and then, as are oval picture frames which are presumably patterned after New England originals. Drinking mugs, some of them in brownware, some with mottlings of green and cream and very rarely a sgraffito-incised one, are found. All of them attest to the originality and skill of industrious potters to whom every bit of prepared clay was something to be put to use.

Another manifestation of Pennsylvania Dutch ingenuity is to be seen in what has come to be called Lehnware, after Joseph Lehn, who, quite late in the nineteenth century, took to ornamented wood turning as a means of livelihood. It is true that his pieces were intended for actual use, but, judging from the condition in which most of them are found, it would appear that few housewives did anything with them which might mar their brilliant colors. Of the hollowed receptacles which constitute his output, the saffron box may be suggested as a first choice. Saffron was primarily intended for coloring butter or noodles. So penetrating is its deep yellow that it had to be handled carefully because of the danger of stains. When not in use it was kept in a closed container out of the way in a high cupboard. Lehn's saffron boxes were footed after the manner of a low goblet, and provided with a domed cover. The typical body coloring was a grayed red, upon which leaves and flowers and frequently strawberries were painted free-hand. The favorite flower was a three-petaled form in red, with a black heart and black-tipped yellow stamens. The green leaves were veined in red, and the stalk was outlined in dark red or black, with a touch of yellow. Concentric circles of black, green, and red were used on the base, the red also appearing at the top of the well-shaped bowl. The inside was usually in yellow, a hue intensified by the saffron. Egg cups, salt boxes, and small bowls of various sizes and shapes followed the same pattern in design and decoration, as did miniature cups and saucers.

The characteristic pink-red of the smaller articles was not used in the larger wooden buckets, another of Lehn's specialties. These pails, expertly coopered, were ordinarily painted red outside and white within. The metal hoops were black, with a continuous wavy line of yellow trailing vine-like around the entire circumference. From the central vine sprouted leaves of green and yellow, with a dab of red at the base of each. Heavy metal tabs anchored the wire bail, which was provided with a turned wooden cylinder at the top for a finger grip. The buckets were of various sizes, but the smaller ones, ranging in capacity from two to six quarts, received detailed decoration not found in the larger vessels. Small wooden tubs with two elongated, pierced staves in place of bails have been found in Lehnware, as well as an occasional ice cream freezer. A covered sugar barrel, twelve inches high from base to brass knob at the top of the cover, is but a variant of these forms. There are a few rare articles in green.

Still other "purely ornamental" articles in wood, in pottery, in metal, and in fabric are to be found in pieces that are one-of-a-kind, but usually such as do not come within the ken of the average collector, and certainly not of the amateur. A study of the books in specialized aspects of the field, supplemented by trips to museums, diligent perusal of auctioneers' and auction gallery catalogues, plus a policy of watchful waiting will pay valuable dividends.

Books

As a finishing touch to the by now Dutch-furnished stone house, it is not improbable that the collector will wish to have at hand some of the myriad books written either by the people themselves or by outsiders who have found them and their way of life interesting. It is possible to build up an extensive and valuable library, and that without paying first edition prices, either.

From the time of Pastorius of Germantown to the present there are five recognizable literary periods in the Dutch country, of varying degrees of interest to the library-builder. The works of the earliest of these periods are largely religious in nature, are principally in German, and cover the years 1683 to 1800. For the most part they were written by the great spiritual leaders of the Colony, men comparable in stature to the better-known New England divines, whose works were in English. The collector who enters this territory will find that while much research has been done and many important titles have been listed, there is not much material of interest except to the serious and patient scholar. This era also includes a considerable number of travel and account books, many of them in English.

Following this time of intense religious activity, there was a period in which the German Pennsylvanians began experimenting with their hitherto purely oral dialect, testing its possibilities as a medium for written literature. From 1800 to about 1860, simultaneously with the decline of interest in high or literary German, newspaper men published various short articles, letters, and verse, and found an eager response in their public. As a cultural experiment it was far more important than the halting results might indicate, for it marked something unique in the world of literature: a conscious and a successful attempt to create a literature where none had previously existed. Only a very small part of this material has been collected in book form.

The third of the five literary periods of the Dutchland has much to offer the collector, for during this time a great deal was written in prose and verse, principally in the dialect. For the few who can read German, mastering the related dialect offers no particular obstacle. For the many who cannot, there are interesting works employing the dialect side by side with English. There are also translations into the dialect of standard English and American literary favorites. Not a few important libraries have been built up by starting with works in this period, which runs from the 1860's to the end of the century.

Interesting but prejudicial are the "outlanders'" works of the era from 1900 to 1928, a time during which the "quaintness" of the Pennsylvania Dutch captured popular fancy. A veritable flood of light fiction, sometimes from the pens of those not too well qualified to write, presented the idiosyncrasies of the Dutch country as representative rather than exceptional. It is largely owing to this widely disseminated fiction that the sturdy citizenry of the lower Pennsylvania counties is so often made the subject of jest today.

The contemporary period is both complex and important. Probably every person who reads at all has read several popular novels having to do with the Dutch country, and perhaps has seen a play or a moving picture with a Pennsylvania background. There are excellent children's books on the market, some of them beautifully illustrated. New and important writers in the dialect are appearing. The researches of historians and scholars have presented facts which make it all but impossible any longer for literary frauds to be foisted on the public. An indigenous drama is an outgrowth of a general recognition of the fact that the cultural heritage of the Dutch country is colorful and unique.

As a starting point merely, and not as an exhaustive list, an annotated bibliography is presented here. The tendency for the average collector, who will undoubtedly have been stimulated by informative articles in current periodicals, is often to start with the more recent works on the market. Any book which will result in a clearer picture of the times, places, and men combining to produce his houseful of treasures will repay the collector many times; but he who does best will supplement his English fiction and non-fiction with at least a sprinkling of the works of those who have used the dialect.

American Collector, The. A periodical popular among collectors.

American-German Review, The. A bi-monthly devoted to German contributions to American living.

Annual *Proceedings* of the Pennsylvania German Society, Norristown, Pennsylvania. These volumes, free to members of the Society, have been published since 1891, and contain unsurpassed source material on German Pennsylvania.

Annual *Publications* of the Pennsylvania German Folklore Society, Fogelsville, Pennsylvania. Free to members, these attractively bound books are authoritative and interesting.

Anonymous, *Two Years behind the Plough.* Philadelphia: Claxton, Remsen & Hafflefinger, 1878. Pp. xii + 224. Light fiction.

Antiques. The "standard" periodical.

Appel, Mrs. T. Roberts. *Old Pennsylvania Recipes*. Lancaster, Pa.: 1933. Pp. 16.

Aurand, A. M. *A Pennsylvania German Library*. Harrisburg, Pa.: Aurand Press, 1930. Pp. 61. A comprehensive listing of Pennsylvania titles. (A complete list of this author's many pamphlets may be obtained by writing to Aurand's Book Store, 900 North Third Street, Harrisburg, Pa.)

——. *Pennsylvania-German Stories and Poems*. Beaver Springs, Pa.: A. M. Aurand, 1916. Pp. 128.

Bahn, Rachel. *Poems*. York, Pa.: H. C. Adams & Co., 1869. Pp. xii + 200. English and dialect; rare.

Balestier, Wolcott. *A Victorious Defeat*. New York: Harper & Bros., 1886. Pp. 349. Fiction. (Out of print.)

Beatty, Charles. *The Journal of a Two Months Tour; with a View of Promoting Religion among the Frontier Inhabitants of Pennsylvania*. London: Davenhill and Pearch, 1768. Pp. 110. Rare.

Beidelman, William. *The Story of the Pennsylvania Germans*. Easton, Pa.: Express Book Print, 1898. Pp. viii + 254. Readable non-fiction. (Out of print.)

Bellamann, Henry. *Floods of Spring*. New York: Simon and Schuster, 1942. Pp. 374. Fiction. Wife of central figure is Pennsylvania Dutch.

Birmelin, John. *Gezwitscher*. Allentown, Pa.: The Pennsylvania German Folklore Society, 1938. Pp. 156. Perhaps the best of all dialect poetry.

Blake, Katharine Evans. *Heart's Haven*. Indianapolis: Bobbs-Merrill, 1905. Pp. 496. Fiction. (Out of print.)

Borneman, Henry S. *Pennsylvania German Illuminated Manuscripts*. Norristown, Pa.: The Pennsylvania German Society, 1937. Beautiful reproductions of fractur in full color.

Budd, Thomas. *Good Order Established in Pennsylvania & New Jersey*. Possibly London: Andrew Sowle, 1685. Extremely rare. Pp. 40.

de Angeli, Marguerite. *Henner's Lydia*. Garden City, N. Y.: Doubleday Doran, 1937. Pp. 70 (unpaged). Excellent juvenile.

——. *Skippack School*. Garden City, N. Y.: Doubleday Doran, 1939. Pp. 86 (unpaged). Excellent juvenile.

de Forest, Marion. *Erstwhile Susan*. New York: Samuel French, 1926. Pp. 114. One of the few plays available in print.

Dorman, William K., and Davidow, L. S. *Pennsylvania Dutch Cook Book of Fine Old Recipes*. Reading, Pa.: Culinary Arts Press, 1934. Pp. vii + 48.

Drepperd, Carl W. *American Pioneer Arts and Artists*. Springfield, Mass.: The Pond-Ekberg Co., 1942. Pp. xiv + 172.

Early American Industries Chronicle, The. A periodical.

Ephrata Brethren, The. *Paradisisches Wunder-Spiel*. Ephrata, Pa.: 1766. Pp. 448. German. An important collector's item; rare. Religious verse.

Falkner, Daniel. *Curieuse Nachricht in Norden America.* Franckfurt und Leipzig: Andreas Otto, 1702. Two double pages + 58. German; rare. An early "travel" book.

Faust, A. B. *The German Element in the United States.* New York: Steuben Society of America, 1927. Pp. xxviii + 730. A full historical treatment.

Fisher, Henry Lee. *Kurzweil un Zeitfertrieb.* York, Pa.: Fischer Brüder, 1882. Pp. 187. Good dialect verse. (Out of print.)

——. *Olden Times: or, Pennsylvania Rural Life Some Fifty Years Ago.* York, Pa.: Fisher Brothers, 1888. Pp. xiv + 472. Excellent genre poetry. (Out of print.)

——. *'S Alt Marik-Haus Mittes in D'r Schtadt* un *Die Alte Zeite.* York, Pa.: The York Republican, 1879. Pp. 273. Well-loved volume of dialect verse. (Out of print.)

Fogel, Edwin M. *Proverbs of the Pennsylvania Germans,* in Pennsylvania German Society *Proceedings,* 1929. Pp. 221. The most important book in its field.

Frederick, J. George. *The Pennsylvania Dutch and Their Cookery.* New York: The Business Bourse, 1935. Pp. 275. Informative and readable.

Frey, J. William. *A Simple Grammar of Pennsylvania Dutch.* Clinton, So. Car.: J. William Frey, 1942. Pp. xi + 140. Invaluable for newcomers to the dialect.

Gibbons, Phebe Earle. *Pennsylvania Dutch and Other Essays.* Philadelphia: J. B. Lippincott & Co., 1874. Pp. 318. An interesting account of Pennsylvania Dutch habits and customs by an outsider. (Out of print.)

Graeff, Arthur D. *The History of Pennsylvania.* Philadelphia: John C. Winston Co., 1944. Pp. 320. Illustrated.

Graydon, Alexander. *Memoirs of a Life Chiefly Passed in Pennsylvania.* Harrisburg, Pa.: John Wyeth, 1811. Pp. 378.

Greensfelder, Elmer. *Broomsticks, Amen!* New York: Longmans, Green & Co., 1932. Pp. 122. A play exploiting English-dialect jargon.

Grumbine, Ezra. *Der Prahl-Hans and Other Rhymes.* Lebanon, Pa.: Sowers Printing Co., 1917. Pp. 113. Dialect.

Grumbine, Lee L. *Der Dengelstock.* Lancaster, Pa.: New Era Printing Press, 1903. Pp. 155. Dialect verse.

Haldeman, S. S. *Pennsylvania Dutch, a Dialect of South Germany with an Infusion of English:* London: Trübner & Co., 1872. Pp. viii + 69. (Rare). Good treatise on the language.

Harbaugh, Henry. *Harbaugh's Harfe.* Philadelphia: B. Bausman, 1870. Pp. 121. The first important collection of dialect poetry, now also available in reprint, Philadelphia: Heidelberg Press, *ca.* 1902. Pp. 120.

Hark, Ann. *Hex Marks the Spot.* Philadelphia and New York: J. B. Lippincott Co., 1938. Pp. 316. A collection of very readable sketches.

——, and DeWitt, C. H. *The Story of the Pennsylvania Dutch.* New York: Harper & Bros., 1943. Pp. 32 (unpaged). A juvenile with excellent lithographs.

Harter, T. H. *Boonastiel.* Bellefonte, Pa.: T. H. Harter, 1904. Pp. 259. Short dialect prose articles. New edition, Harrisburg, Pa.: Aurand Press, 1942, with introduction and biographical sketch by A. M. Aurand, Jr.

Heckman, Oliver S. *What to Read about Pennsylvania.* Harrisburg, Pa.: Pennsylvania Historical Commission, 1942. Pp. vii + 97. Good bibliography.

Hergesheimer, Joseph. *The Foolscap Rose.* New York: Alfred A. Knopf, 1934. Pp. 312. Fiction.

——. *Three Black Pennys.* New York: Alfred A. Knopf, 1917. Pp. 408. A tale of the Welsh Mountain.

Hildeburn, Charles S. *A Century of Printing, 1685-1776.* Philadelphia: Matlack and Harvey, 1885. Pp. xx + 908. (2 vols.) A monumental study. (*See also* Metzger, Ethel Myra.)

Hohman, John George. *Albertus Magnus, der lang verborgenen Schatz und Haus-Freund.* Pennsylvania, 1839. Pp. 100. The original "hex" book. New edition, Harrisburg, Pa.: Aurand Press, 1930. Pp. 94.

Hoover, Francis T. *Enemies in the Rear; or, A Golden Circle Squared.* Boston: Arena Publishing Co., 1895. Pp. xiii + 604. Fiction. (Out of print.)

Horne, A. R. *A Pennsylvania German Manual.* Kutztown, Pa.: Urick & Gehring, 1875. Pp. 172. Parallel dialect and English "grammar"; a valuable book.

Iobst, Clarence F. *En Quart Millich un En Halb Beint Raahm.* Allentown, Pa.: Pennsylvania German Folklore Society, 1939. Pp. 63. Best known of the contemporary dialect plays.

Jordan, Mildred. *Apple in the Attic.* New York: Alfred A. Knopf, 1942. Pp. xi + 200. Fiction.

——. *One Red Rose Forever.* New York: Alfred A. Knopf, 1941. Pp. 550. A fictional presentation of the affairs of "Baron" Stiegel.

——. *Shoo-Fly Pie.* New York: Alfred A. Knopf, 1944. Pp. 118. Juvenile.

Kauffman, Reginald W. *The House of Bondage.* New York: Moffat, Yard, & Co., 1910. Pp. 466. Fiction. (Out of print.)

Keller, David. *The Devil and the Doctor.* New York: Simon and Schuster, 1940. Pp. 308. Light fiction with minor Pennsylvania Dutch characters.

Keyser, Mrs. C. Naaman. *Home Craft Courses.* Plymouth Meeting, Pa.: Mrs. C. Naaman Keyser. A series of pamphlets by Mrs. Keyser and others, for those interested in Pennsylvania Dutch art forms. List of pamphlets available from publisher.

Klosz, Heinz. *Die pennsylvaniadeutsche Literatur.* Munich: Der Deutsche Akademie, 1931. Heft IV, pp. 230–72. German; a good study.

——. *Lewendiche Schtimme aus Pennsilveni*. Stuttgart und New York: B. Westerman, 1929. Pp. 153. A collection of dialect works.

Koons, Ulysses S. *Brother Jabez: a Tale of the Kloster*. Philadelphia: Griffith and Rowland, 1904. Pp. xvi + 336. Fiction. (Out of print.)

Kuhns, Oscar. *German and Swiss Settlements of Pennsylvania*. New York: Henry Holt, 1900. Pp. v + 268. A good study. (Out of print.)

Lambert, Marcus B. *A Dictionary of the Non-English Words of the Pennsylvania-German Dialect*. Norristown, Pa.: The Pennsylvania German Society, 1924. Pp. xxxi + 193. The most comprehensive dictionary; invaluable for the beginner.

Langdon, William Chauncy. *Everyday Things in American Life*. New York: Charles Scribner's Sons, 1939. Pp. xx + 353. Good on Pennsylvania.

Learned, Marion Dexter. *The Pennsylvania-German Dialect*. Baltimore: Isaac Friedenthal, 1889. Pp. 114. Early dictionary. (Out of print.)

Light, Joseph H. *Der Alt Schuhlmeshter*. Lebanon, Pa.: Frank G. Light, 1928. P. 128. Dialect prose.

Lins, James C. *A Commonsense Pennsylvania German Dictionary*. Reading, Pa.: James C. Lins, 1887. Pp. 170. (Out of print.)

Lippard, George. *Paul Ardenheim, the Monk of the Wissahikon*. Philadelphia: T. B. Peterson & Bros., 1848. Pp. 536. Gothic fiction rampant; scarce.

Martin, Helen R. *Tillie: a Mennonite Maid*. New York: Century, 1904. Pp. 336 + viii. One of almost forty works of light fiction by the same author emphasizing the oddities of the Pennsylvania Dutch.

Metzger, Ethel Myra. "Supplement to Hildeburn's Century of Printing, 1685–1775." Columbia University Master's Thesis, 1930. Pp. 126. An important addition to Hildeburn, which see.

Meynen, Emil. *Bibliography on German Settlements in Colonial North America*. Leipzig: Otto Harrassowitz, 1937. Pp. xxxvi + 636. Important work for the serious student.

Milhous, Katherine. *Lovina, a Story of the Amish*. New York: Charles Scribner's Sons, 1940. Pp. 50 (unpaged). Good juvenile.

Miller, Daniel. *Pennsylvania German*, Vol. I. Reading, Pa.: Daniel Miller, 1903. Pp. viii + 292. Good collection of short works in the dialect. (Out of print.)

——. *Pennsylvania German*, Vol. II. Reading, Pa.: Daniel Miller, 1911. Pp. vii + 265. (Out of print.)

Miller, Harvey. *G'shbos und Arnsht*. Elizabethville, Pa.: Hawthorne Press, 1939. Pp. 384. Dialect verse.

——. *Pennsylvania German Poems*. Elizabethville, Pa.: Hawthorne Press, 1906. Pp. 116.

Mittelberger, Gottlieb. *Reise nach Pennsylvanien im Jahr 1750 und Rückreise nach Teutschland im Jahr 1754*. Stuttgart: Gottlieb Friderich Jenisch, 1756. Pp. 120. German; rare.

Mortimer, Charlotte B. *Bethlehem and Bethlehem School*. New York: Stanford & Delisser, 1858. Pp. 208. Reminiscences. (Out of print.)

——. *Marrying by Lot*. New York: Putnam & Sons, 1868. Pp. xi + 405. An account of an early Moravian custom. (Out of print.)

Moss, Alfred Charles. *Pinafore*. Allentown, Pa.: G. C. Aschbach & Co., 1882. Pp. 20. Gilbert and Sullivan in the dialect; a collector's item par excellence.

Myers, Anna Balmer. *Patchwork, a Story of the Plain People*. Philadelphia: George W. Jacobs & Co., 1920. Pp. 338. Light fiction. (Out of print.)

Myers, Elizabeth L. *A Century of Moravian Sisters*. New York: Fleming H. Revell, 1918. Pp. 243. Interesting customs explained.

Ogden, John C. *An Excursion into Bethlehem & Nazareth in the Year 1799*. Philadelphia: Charles Cist, 1800. Pp. 167. Rare.

Pastorius, Francis Daniel, *Kurtze Geographische Beschreibung der letztmals erfundenen Amerikanischen Landsschafft Pensylvania*. Nürnberg: Christian Sigmund Froberg, 1692. Pp. 32. German; excellent but rare.

——. *Umständige Geographische Beschreibung der zu allerletzt erfundenen Provintz Pennsylvaniae*. Frankfurt und Leipzig: Andreas Otto, 1704. Pp. 6 double pages + 140. German; rare.

Pattee, Fred Lewis. *The House of the Black Ring*. New York: Henry Holt & Co., 1905. Pp. v + 324. Fiction.

Pennsylvania German Magazine, The. An important periodical which suspended publication in 1914. Numbers are now collector's items.

Proud, Robert. *The History of Pennsylvania in North America*. Philadelphia: Zachariah Poulson, Jr., 1797. Vol. I, 1797, pp. 508; Vol. II, 1798, pp. 373 + 146. Scarce.

Rauch, E. H. *De Campain Breefa fum Pit Schweffelbrenner un de Bevy, Si Alty*. Lancaster, Pa.: Rauch & Cochran, 1868. Pp. 45. Dialect prose articles. (Out of print.)

——. *Pennsylvania Dutch Hand-Book*. Mauch Chunk, Pa.: E. H. Rauch, 1879. Pp. 238. A study of the language. (Out of print.)

——. *The Pennsylvania Dutchman*. Lancaster, Pa.: Wylie & Griest, 1873. Important, rare early periodical. Only three numbers are known, those for January, February, and March, 1873.

Reichard, Harry Hess. *Pennsylvania German Dialect Writings and Their Writers*, in Pennsylvania German Society *Proceedings*, 1915. Pp. 400. The most important work in its field.

——. *Pennsylvania German Verse*, in Pennsylvania German Society *Proceedings*, 1940. Pp. 299. An anthology.

Rhoads, J. N. *A Thunderstorm*. Philadelphia: Ferris & Leach, 1904. Pp. 296. Fiction.

Rhoads, Thomas J. B. *Onkel Jeff's Reminiscences of Youth and Other Poems.*
Williamsport, Pa.: T. J. B. Rhoads, 1904. Pp. 2 + 9 + 399.

Riccardi, Saro John. *Pennsylvania Dutch Folk Art and Architecture.* New York:
The New York Public Library, 1942. Pp. 15. A superlative bibliography in its field, and invaluable to every collector.

Richter, Conrad. *The Free Man.* New York: Alfred Knopf, 1943. Pp.
viii + 147. One of the best of recent novels.

Robacker, Earl F. *Pennsylvania German Literature.* Philadelphia: The University of Pennsylvania Press, 1943. Pp. x + 217. Covers dialect,
German, and English prose and verse from 1683 to 1942, with full
bibliography.

Rush, Benjamin. *An Account of the Manners of the German Inhabitants of Pennsylvania.* Reprinted in Pennsylvania German Society *Proceedings*, 1910,
by Theodore E. Schmauk. Pp. 128.

Sachse, Julius F., *The German Pietists of Provincial Pennsylvania.* Philadelphia:
P. C. Stockhausen, 1895. Pp. xviii + 504. Source book; scarce.

——. *The German Sectarians of Pennsylvania.* Philadelphia: P. C. Stockhausen, 1900. Pp. xvi + 535. Source book; scarce.

Saur, Christopher, *Ein Geistliches Magazien.* Germantown, Pa.: Christopher
Saur, 1764. Pp. iv + 406. German; extremely rare.

Schlosser, Ralph W. *The Court Scene from The Merchant of Venice Translated
into the Pennsylvania German Dialect.* Elizabethtown, Pa.: Elizabethtown
College, 1940. Pp. 15.

Schock, Georg. *Hearts Contending.* New York: Harper & Bros., 1910.
Pp. 272. Fiction. (Out of print.)

——. *The House of Yost.* New York: Boni and Liveright, 1923. Pp. 310.
Fiction. (Out of print.)

Seidensticker, Oswald. *The First Century of German Printing in America, 1728–
1830.* Philadelphia: Schafer & Koradi, 1893. Pp. x + 253. Good
bibliography. (Out of print.)

Seyfert, Ella Maie. *Amish Moving Day.* New York: Thomas Y. Crowell,
1942. Pp. 126. Juvenile.

Singmaster, Elsie. *A High Wind Rising.* Boston: Houghton Mifflin, 1942.
Pp. viii + 296. Historical fiction of Revolutionary times.

——. *Bred in the Bone, and Other Stories.* New York: Houghton Mifflin, 1925.
Pp. 300. Good collection of short stories.

——. *The Magic Mirror.* New York: Houghton Mifflin, 1934. Pp. 284.
One of the best novels on Pennsylvania Dutch manners and life.

——. *When Sarah Saved the Day.* Boston and New York: Houghton Mifflin,
1909. Pp. 135. Juvenile.

Sixth and Seventh Book of Moses. New York: Empire Publishing Co., 1938.
Pp. 128. One of the old, forbidden "hex" books, reprinted.

'*S Pennsylfawnisch Deitsch Eck.* A regular feature in the Saturday Allentown, Pennsylvania "Morning Call." Edited by Dr. Preston A. Barba, it is probably the most important contemporary contribution to the literature and lore of the Pennsylvania Germans. This feature is available in a reprint.

Steckel, A. D. *Dumhete.* Fullerton, Pa.: Stutzman Printing Co., 1930. Pp. 36, (unpaged). Dialect articles. (Out of print.)

Stoudt, John Baer. *The Folklore of the Pennsylvania-German.* Supplement to Pennsylvania German Society *Proceedings*, 1915. Pp. 155.

Thomas, Edith M. *Mary at the Farm and Book of Recipes.* Harrisburg, Pa.: Evangelical Press, 1915. Pp. 423. Fiction and cookery.

Thomas, Gabriel. *An Historical and Geographical Account of the Province and Country of Pensilvania and of West-New Jersey in America.* London: A. Baldwin, 1698. Pp. 7 (unpaged) + 55. Rare.

Trexler, B. F. *Skizzen aus dem Lecha-Thale.* Allentown, Pa.: Trexler & Hartzell, 1880–86. Pp. 260. German and dialect; a good source book, but scarce.

Troxell, William S., *Aus Pennsylfawnia.* Philadelphia: The University of Pennsylvania Press, 1938. Pp. xiii + 47. A beginner's "must"; parallel pages in English and dialect from "Hamlet" to "The Night before Christmas." (Out of print.)

Walters, Raube. *The Hex Woman.* New York: The Macaulay Co., 1931. Pp. 320. Fiction. (Out of print.)

Warner, Joseph H. *Amerikanisch Historie.* Annville, Pa.: Journal Publishing Co., 1905. Pp. vii + 100. Amusing satire in the dialect. (Out of print.)

Weitzel, Louisa. *Shpectakel.* Lititz, Pa.: Record Printing Co., 1931. Pp. 36. Dialect verse. (Out of print.)

Wertenbaker, Thomas J. *The Founding of American Civilization: The Middle Colonies.* New York: Charles Scribner's Sons, 1938. Pp. xiii + 367. A good historical treatment.

Weygandt, Cornelius J. *A Passing America.* New York: Henry Holt & Co., 1932. Pp. xxi + 330. The sketches and essays in all the Weygandt books are eminently readable.

——. *Philadelphia Folks.* New York: D. Appleton-Century Co., 1938. Pp. xx + 357.

——. *The Blue Hills.* New York: Henry Holt & Co., 1936. Pp. xx + 434.

——. *The Dutch Country.* New York: D. Appleton-Century Co., 1939. Pp. xx + 352.

——. *The Plenty of Pennsylvania.* New York: H. C. Kinsey & Co., 1942. Pp. x + 319.

——. *The Red Hills*. Philadelphia: The University of Pennsylvania Press, 1929. Pp. xi + 251. The antique hunter's Bible, but out of print at present.

——. *The Wissahickon Hills*. Philadelphia: The University of Pennsylvania Press, 1930. Pp. xiii + 366.

Williamson, Thames. *D Is for Dutch*. New York: Harcourt, Brace & Co., 1934. Pp. 266. Fiction.

Wollenweber, Ludwig A. *Aus Berks County's Schwerer Zeit*. Reading, Pa.: W. Rosenthal, 1875. Pp. 40. Dialect.

——. *Gemaelde aus dem Pennsylvanischen Volksleben*. Philadelphia: Schafer und Koradi, 1869. Pp. 143. Word pictures of life in Pennsylvania. (Out of print).

——. *Treu Bis in der Tod*. Philadelphia: Ig. Kohler, 1880. Pp. 68. A dialect romance. (Out of print.)

——. *Zwei Treue Kameraden*. Philadelphia: Ig. Kohler, 1882. Pp. 72. Dialect tale. (Out of print.)

Wood, Ralph, editor. *The Pennsylvania Germans*. Princeton, N. J.: Princeton University Press, 1942. Pp. viii + 299. A collection of informative articles by eminent professional men.

Yoder, Joseph W. *Rosanna of the Amish*. Huntingdon, Pa.: Yoder Publishing Co., 1940. Pp. 319. A distinctive tale reading like fiction.

Ziegler, Charles Calvin. *Drauss un Deheem*. Allentown, Pa.: The Pennsylvania German Folklore Society, 1936. Pp. 73. Good dialect poetry.

Zimmerman, Thomas C., *Olla Podrida*. Reading, Pa.: Times Publishing Co., 1903. Pp. 220. Dialect sketches. (Out of print.)

Contemporary Dutch

THERE are those who like the fine flavor of the good things of the past but who are handicapped in securing them, or who have no particular desire to collect or to own the originals. Others, whose homes are subject to hard everyday living, think of the havoc that can be caused by just one children's party and decide that the sensible thing to do is to steer clear of fragile plaster ornaments, easily gouged soft wood, textiles that must be treated with gentle courtesy, and the like. For these persons there may be a vicarious satisfaction in the reproductions and imitations that have sprung into existence almost spontaneously of recent years.

Seldom will one who genuinely loves antiques admit any good in a reproduction. He has become so accustomed to watching for fakes and evidences of spuriousness that anything smacking of imitation becomes anathema to him. Yet the age checks, the chips and the cracks, the worn surface, the warped line, and the broken member that offend him so little may be strongly distasteful to many who admire the perfection of the old but want it brand new and untouched by previous associations. The dower chest rescued from the chicken coop, while it would delight the heart of almost any collector, would be nothing but a cause for consternation to many whose liking for painted and decorated furniture is unquestioned and whose taste in home decoration is impeccable. Obviously, then, there should be no occasion for lifted eyebrows when Mrs. Jones sallies forth to the department store to acquire the betuliped object which reminds her of what she saw in the American Wing at the Metropolitan. A good reproduction is a flattering commentary on the original—as long as it retains its status as a reproduction.

Not all reproductions are good, and some few are very bad. Those that are good tend to follow the line and color of the original, and in the same manner and proportion as the original. Those which borrow a single motif, such as the heart or the tulip, and then conventionalize it beyond resemblance to the original are usually bad. So are those which use a deliberately crude technique, a falsification of colors, and an application of design to surfaces never intended to be other than plain. Very questionable are those which tend to utilize as many different motifs as possible on one single object, a favorite stunt among commercial artists who should know better. When generalization sets in, the real beauty of Pennsylvania Dutch work is lost.

There is good contemporary pottery to be had, but it is not yet being produced extensively and is little known outside of Pennsylvania. Following the ways of the old potters, Mrs. Naaman Keyser, of Plymouth Meeting, Pa., has reproduced the old designs in the traditional pieces mentioned earlier in this work. This new-old ware has met with general approval among those to whom quality is important and age irrelevant. Brochures by the artist about her work are indicated in the chapter on books. The products of the Stahl brothers and of Jacob Medinger have been mentioned earlier.

In the department stores one may find a kind of pottery in a light cream tone, with a single profile tulip reminiscent of those of the Ephrata fractur work; that is, with the petals widely separated. The colors are red and green. Pieces noted include candlesticks, a variety of oval and square low bowls and objects for mantel garniture. It is good in workmanship and design, but not particularly Pennsylvania Dutch, except for the borrowed tulip.

A few years ago a maker of tea tiles conceived the idea of using Pennsylvania Dutch motifs, apparently without realizing that similar tiles had long been popular with collectors, who used them, among other purposes, in reconstructing fireplaces. The *distelfink* or goldfinch, the tulip, the rose, and the tree of life designs were all employed. More recently some of the tiles imported from Holland by the early settlers were copied and placed on the market. As reproductions these were generally meritorious. Sophisticated but less authentic in effect is the work offered by some of the smart gift shops, for the designs are highly conventionalized, and often wispy or wraithlike. Frequently these tiles go by sets, as in the case of a square of nine, the component parts forming a single pattern, with the whole embedded in the wooden top of a coffee table.

Considerably less expensive than the foregoing are modern imitations of spatterware. Some of the Southern mountain potteries are turning out, on a commercial scale, salad plates and bowls, tea sets and occasional odd pieces like salad forks and spoons and relish dishes, all with spattered edges, usually green. These are of good quality. No effort has been made to imitate the important designs of spatterware, the basic ornamentation oftenest consisting of single or clustered fruits in color. Definitely cheap in quality and imitative as to design are eight-inch round open bowls with spattered edges and an Adams rose at the center. Similarly shaped and spattered bowls are also found with large central blooms in strong colors, not unattractive in their way. Red spatter tea sets with a large, many-petaled red flower as the center of interest have been offered for sale in the past few years.

Chinaware for table settings in the feeling of the Pennsylvania Dutch, and probably suggested by bona fide designs, include decorations of tulips, of roses, of hearts, and of birds enough like *distelfinks* to be called *distelfinks*. Both color and pattern are good, and the price is not unreasonable.

Pattern glass reproductions are less innocent, since steadily rising prices have proved a stimulus to imitators, who have palmed off their spurious wares as the genuine article. A standard work by an authority in the field, a work kept up to date by frequent supplements, has proved valuable to those interested in glass. Offered for sale without any attempt at fooling the public are daisy and button glass objects in various colors including pink, opalescent, pale blue, amber, and vaseline, and a considerable variety of bottles, vases, bowls, and jars in hobnail. Blue and cranberry red are particularly popular here. Mexican glass is so well known that it hardly calls for comment, except to remind the reader that there is a rather wider range in color than the beginner who is accustomed to the familiar dark blue would at first suppose. Where special color effects are desired it has much to offer. There are various tones ranging from clear through light green, through a whole galaxy of blues, and various ambers, purple, and puce. The shapes of plates and cups, cruets and bottles do not always approximate those of the United States, but pitchers, tumblers, and jugs are often so like Stiegel pieces that now and then they have puzzled the experts. Of late, small pitchers and various bottles, consciously patterned after Stiegel and South Jersey, have appeared in the stores, especially the gift shops. These are of American make, and are tagged by their trade names. Most attractive are those in purple and in a clear dark green.

Enameled glass bottles are offered for sale, not especially like those of Stiegel and with no apparent attempt at copying, but close enough to use where a Pennsylvania Dutch atmosphere is to be suggested.

There seems to be an almost wholesale return to favor of milk glass, not only in the bureau pieces, setting hens, and pin trays of memory, but of new shapes and sizes. Many of these are so gilded and covered with roses and forget-me-nots that it might almost seem that the Victorians were once more with us. A small lamp with both the oil reservoir and the glass chimney fairly plastered with decalcomania flowers is a case in point. A great impetus to the popularity of this type of thing was given when one of the large city department stores amassed a tremendous number of the more awkward and cumbersome pieces of furniture of the Victorian period, cut them up, reassembled them, painted them in pink and white and sold them to the public, if not "with bells on," according to the old adage, at least with ribbons on. Like begets like, and as long as people consent to live with these pink and white elephants the gift shops will provide things to go with them.

In furniture there are some fine reproductions showing Pennsylvania Dutch influence. There is a modern version of the dower chest in particular (costing almost as much as an attested original, by the way) which follows its country ancestor closely in line and proportion. The colors, however, while harmonious, are less striking than the Pennsylvania Dutch would have approved. Other dower chests that are faithful copies of museum pieces have also lately appeared in the stores. Outstanding are those in the old Pennsylvania gray-blue and others in red and black. It is also to be noted that there are fine old chests which have been newly decorated for resale. Neither completely old nor completely new, they serve very neatly as transitional pieces when, as is generally the case, they have been treated with good taste.

One of the first Pennsylvania Dutch pieces to be reproduced for the public was the dough tray or kneading box mounted on legs. This was decorated in panels after the fashion of one in a museum, and is a very handy article of furniture, even if rather far removed from its original purpose. No one has yet provided a more convenient receptacle for periodicals and papers.

Low post beds in spool design as well as those with corner finials of pleasing shape are commonly found, usually in light-toned woods such as maple and pine. Birch, seldom used for furniture in the Dutch country, has been used to good effect in reproductions.

Small wooden objects with applied Pennsylvania Dutch ornamentation are found every now and then. One is a case for stationery, and another a spice box. Besides these there are boxes with heart, angel, or bird decoration in good approximations of the originals. Colorful salad bowls with heart and tulip are to be had—at a very fancy figure.

The bucket bench, so characteristic of rural Pennsylvania furniture, has been reproduced, and painted and decorated beyond anything that the early settlers knew about but the result is pleasing and quite at home with other painted furniture. Also to be found in stores are knife boxes (frequently adapted for use as highball trays), corner wall brackets, straight chairs and rocking chairs, churns (used as floor lamp bases), low chests of drawers and small chests, bearing hearts, birds, flowers, angels or all of them, in shapes and proportions suggestive of the best in Pennsylvania Dutch artistry. Some of them are Swedish in inspiration, some Viennese, but all show a degree of kinship close enough to enable them to fraternize comfortably. Noteworthy among boldly painted pieces of American furniture of this type are those by Peter Hunt.

It is in the field of painted tôle that the old-versus-new idea in Pennsylvania Dutch decoration comes closest to the point of controversy. The supply of fine originals was almost exhausted before the demand had really begun, but there were many trays, herb pots, spice boxes, and other objects which were in good condition except for their floral patterns, or which had never been ornamented at all. It was almost inevitable that sooner or later someone would do over the old pieces and put them on the market. Whether it would have been better to imitate the designs and colors of the genuine article exactly than to "improve" upon the originals is a moot point, but there is at present before the public a somewhat bewildering array of painted tin—bewildering because some of it is old, some old with new designs, some new with old designs, and some completely new but looking old. If one wishes for tulip decoration, he may buy it on sugar scoops, watering pots, coffee grinders, trays of many sizes and shapes, and a dozen other objects or utensils which were innocent of any decoration in the good old days. Still, it is actually the old tin, if there is either merit or consolation in that fact. The decoration is usually markedly stylized, according to the interpretation of the artist, who may have a predilection for yellow or a penchant for pansies. In other cases, new objects of tinware, such as canister sets and lamp bases, are painted imaginatively and colorfully, and if anyone wishes to buy them for Pennsylvania Dutch he will have no difficulty in finding a clerk who will eagerly assure him that they are just that. This is about on a par with the practice of furbishing up a piece of old tinware, putting a tulip on it and then offering it as a genuine antique.

Really good in modern tôleware are floor lamps in green, blue, red, yellow, and antique ivory. Well designed and proportioned, and with a minimum of decorative detail, they harmonize with almost any interior, whether contemporary or traditional.

Now and then, among the shiny Mexican tinware of the department stores one will come across a candle sconce or a plate which will go well with the Pennsylvania ornamentation. Generally, however, these are too bright, except as one may feel the need for a single piece as an accent. Mexican baskets, also, when not too liberally painted in red, purple, and green, sometimes suggest the earlier baskets of Pennsylvania.

The dearth of genuine fabrics of the Painted Period has been responsible for a considerable number of Pennsylvania Dutch designs, so called, in linen and in fabrics which have a rough texture or a homespun effect. Many of these were designed for table cloths, and one of them, a hand-blocked cotton, is so arranged that it can be cut into squares of napkin size. Some are hand-loomed in authentic reproductions of the brown or blue gingham-like material popular with country housewives. Useful and popular, especially for dining room use, are white fabrics blocked in simple red cherry and strawberry designs. One of the outstanding achievements of the past decade is Tony Sarg's "Stone House" cotton fabric, with its recurring motifs of dower chest, tree of life, tulip, bird, heart, coffee pot, sgraffito plate, and others. This material was marketed as yard goods, and was also made up into cushions, lamp shades, and in other ways.

The vogue for the old decoration has extended even to objects of paper, such as lamp shades, paper napkins, and place mats. These generally feature Pennsylvania Dutch boys and girls, with the other parts of the design more or less conventionalized. A well-known manufacturer has produced a wall paper using a Pennsylvania Dutch design, and there is also a wall paper border in a bird pattern, for use over oil-painted surfaces. Very recently a set of ten different artist's sketches of representative scenes in the Dutch country was placed on the market in the form of greeting cards. Never let it be said that the world has by-passed the back country of Pennsylvania. If ever the world made a beaten track to anyone's door, it was to the door of the Pennsylvania Dutchman's stone house!

For those who would achieve authentic effects without the actual use of antiques a few suggestions as to color may not come amiss. Remember the saying attributed to the Dutchman: "I like any color as long as it's red." The best red would perhaps be vermilion, but no bright red would be wrong. A bright yellow would probably rate second, with blue a close third. These primary hues are to be found over and over, and with a modicum of good judgment the home decorator can work out a satisfactory plan for using them. Green and brown, considerably grayed, can be used to advantage.

A good starting point would be to acquire one well-liked piece, perhaps a dower chest or a bucket bench or a tôle tray, and study the use of color found on it. From that one could determine what color he wished to use for the walls, for the floor covering, for draperies, and for accents. A certain painted chair comes to mind as a keynote for a color scheme: It is of dark brown wood, with a floral and fruit design consisting of bright red cherries, softer red roses fading off into pink, dark green foliage, and creamy yellow dogwood flowers. Narrow bands of black and of yellow frame the decorated portions. The room built around this chair might have cream-colored walls (rough-textured for the best effect), a brown rug, and draperies or upholstery or both in a rose design similar to that of the chair. Either green or yellow tôle lamps and a matching tôle tray might be used with them. Again, a woven coverlet might provide the inspiration, if its dark blue, off-white and muted madder red guided one's selection of paint, furniture, and fabrics.

Even so striking a piece as a black tôle tray in the bird of paradise pattern could be used to establish the color scheme of a room. The colors here would be rose-red, gold, green, and cream, with minor touches of purple and blue. One of the black and red dower chests recently put on the market; draperies of plain red or yellow; a painted chair or two in which yellow or red are prominent; a hooked or braided rug in which all these colors figure but in which red or black is predominant—these would satisfy the demands of good taste and at the same time provide an integrated Pennsylvania Dutch décor.

Museum Collections

BEGINNERS, who often receive the impetus to collect by attending antique shows or shops, or who find their friends' enthusiasm for antiques contagious, will sooner or later find it expedient to visit the fine collections assembled in museums. No matter how assiduously the collector may study books, periodicals, or newspaper features dealing with his field of interest, he can hardly acquire a thorough background without actually seeing the examples that have been found meritorious enough for preservation by the museums and historical societies. The list which follows, suggestive rather than comprehensive, should prove helpful.

The PHILADELPHIA MUSEUM OF ART has one of the outstanding collections in the country. Wall and window treatments are noteworthy; the collection of fireplace implements and utensils is outstanding. The woodwork used was taken from an old house ("The House of the Miller") at Millbach, Pennsylvania, and the staircase in particular is a prime example of craftsmanship. Examples of very early furniture are unsurpassed, although the collector who is looking for specimens of the Painted Period will do better to visit collections which are less highly selective, or which extend more nearly to contemporary times. Good examples of fractur and lighting devices are shown, as well as pottery that includes some of the finest sgraffito in existence.

Of major importance also are the Pennsylvania German rooms in the American Wing of the METROPOLITAN MUSEUM OF ART, New York City. Like those of the Philadelphia Museum of Art, they serve as a background for superior and authentic pieces. The visitor here will see the old gray-blue paint of Pennsylvania used to excellent advantage. Splendid dower chests, candle boxes, bride's boxes, and other painted pieces compete in interest with painted tin, fractur, chalk ornaments, spatterware, Gaudy Dutch, and fine pottery.

One of the most comprehensive collections in the country is that of the BUCKS COUNTY HISTORICAL SOCIETY in Doylestown, Pennsylvania. The five-story building which houses it is unique in construction, the various display rooms facing a central well which extends from floor to roof. The aim has

155

been to preserve examples of each of the tools, implements, or objects used in all the early industries and occupations of Pennsylvania. A great number of cumbersome pieces have been suspended in air about the central well, among them a Conestoga wagon. The collection is by no means confined to German Pennsylvania alone, but includes objects used by various racial strains in the Commonwealth. The visitor will require several days to do justice to the examples assembled. The collection of cast iron stove plates, many of them from the furnaces of "Baron" Stiegel, is probably the best in existence.

Likewise comprehensive in scope is the LANDIS VALLEY MUSEUM, near Lancaster, Pennsylvania. Henry K. Landis, one of the founders, is of the opinion that a satisfactory picture of the past can be gained, not from a study of the finest work alone, but from concentrating on all the examples, good and bad, that have come down to present times. The collection, therefore, shows considerable variation in quality, but is of paramount importance. It is somewhat difficult to single out for comment any particular sections from an assemblage so all-embracing, but there are excellent specimens of painted furniture, tôleware, iron, brass, and copper implements and utensils, cooky cutters, pottery, and guns. A good picture of early domestic industries is to be gained by a visit to the museum.

Outstanding also in Pennsylvania German items is the HERSHEY MUSEUM, Hershey, Pennsylvania. Of particular interest is the excellent Stiegel glass, much of which came from the collection of the late George M. Danner in Manheim, Pennsylvania. Model rooms authentically furnished are an interesting feature of the museum. Early chinaware, including examples of spatterware, Gaudy Dutch, and historical and pictorial Staffordshire, is noteworthy. The unique "Apostle" clock (about which information may be obtained by writing to the museum) is another interesting feature, as is an early music box utilizing large perforated metal discs suggestive of oversized phonograph records.

The HISTORICAL SOCIETY OF PENNSYLVANIA, Philadelphia, is especially noted for its early manuscripts, letters, documents, and books. So comprehensive is the collection that after many years there is still much work to be done in assembling material for the use of scholars and research workers. Material from the time of Benjamin Franklin, Andrew Bradford, and Christopher Saur, among others, is available. The visitor, who would presumably be interested primarily in literary research, might also be impressed by the fine tall case clocks in the various rooms.

Those concerned with early architecture will find the buildings of the CLOISTERS, at Ephrata, Pennsylvania, dating from the early eighteenth century, of signal importance. While not all of the original buildings are still in existence, the Sister House, the Saal, and buildings used as bake-houses and the like are intact. In particular, the fireplaces, narrow passages, doorways, and winding stairways of the Sister House command attention. Crude furniture and old pottery are found in some of the rooms. Most interesting of all are the specimens of illuminated writings shown. Unsur-passed by anything of like nature done in the Colonies, these recall the days when the Cloisters were a center of spiritual life. A few carefully preserved books are all that remain to remind the visitor of the once prolific printing industry that flourished almost as late as Revolutionary times. The build-ings are now under the protection of the Commonwealth.

The NEW YORK HISTORICAL SOCIETY in New York City has an extensive collection of Pennsylvania Dutchiana, effectively displayed. There are good specimens of chalk ornaments, carved butter molds, punched tin, spatter-ware, Gaudy Dutch, King's- and Queen's-Rose china, and furniture. Worthy of special mention are Schimmel wood carvings, and specimens of pioneer American art forms. The MUSEUM OF MODERN ART in New York City also occasionally displays examples of early art forms, among them Pennsylvania Dutch pieces.

The NATIONAL FOLK ARTS SOCIETY in New York City frequently arranges exhibitions of fine Pennsylvania Dutch work. The displays, which are changed from time to time, have included excellent examples of needlework, furniture, pottery, and many small items in which decorative patterns and motifs are emphasized. Many of these have been loan exhibits.

The Archives Building of MORAVIAN COLLEGE AND THEOLOGICAL SEM-INARY, Bethlehem, Pennsylvania, not only has an excellent collection of books, including early imprints, but also some fine furniture. The college itself and the Moravian College for Women have good examples of early furniture as well. Of interest to the historically-minded are the rooms of the MORAVIAN HISTORICAL SOCIETY at Nazareth, Pennsylvania.

The SCHWENKFELDER HISTORICAL SOCIETY, Pennsburg, Pennsylvania, has a valuable collection of the illuminated writings of Christopher Dock, early schoolmaster of the Perkiomen region, as well as other interesting papers and books. There is also a display of basketry, pottery, china, and other me-mentos of the Schwenkfelder sect.

Among other Pennsylvania historical societies which have either perma-nent or loan exhibits are the LANCASTER COUNTY HISTORICAL SOCIETY, Lancaster; the GERMANTOWN HISTORICAL SOCIETY, Philadelphia; the LEHIGH COUNTY HISTORICAL SOCIETY, Allentown; the LEBANON COUNTY HISTORICAL SOCIETY, Lebanon; the HISTORICAL SOCIETY OF MONTGOMERY COUNTY,

Norristown; the HISTORICAL SOCIETY OF YORK COUNTY, York; the HISTORICAL SOCIETY and the READING PUBLIC MUSEUM AND ART GALLERY, Reading; the MONROE COUNTY HISTORICAL SOCIETY, Stroudsburg; and the DAUPHIN COUNTY HISTORICAL SOCIETY, Harrisburg. Also located in Harrisburg are the FORT HUNTER MUSEUM (private) and the PENNSYLVANIA STATE LIBRARY and MUSEUM, which contain Pennsylvania German relics.

Index